Sexuality and Intellectual Disabilities

This book provides a concise overview of sexuality and gender identity in clients with intellectual disabilities for therapists, social workers, educators, and healthcare providers. It captures the social, political, and legal environment of the late 2010s and bridges the gap between research and practice, with engaging case examples drawn from the author's own practice. Guidance on everyday issues, including dating and sex education, is juxtaposed with material on complex, current issues in topics like LGBTQ inclusion and sexual offending. User-friendly "toolboxes" provide brief guides to practical issues such as using trans-friendly language and providing family interventions. Accessible enough for students and trainees, but thorough enough for veteran clinicians, this book explores issues that professionals face in providing competent care through the lens of justice and inclusion.

Andrew Maxwell Triska, MSW, is a social worker and therapist who currently practices in the inpatient psychiatric unit at New York-Presbyterian Brooklyn Methodist Hospital, consults on gender and sexuality topics, and develops materials for social work textbooks. He received his MSW from the Silberman School of Social Work at Hunter College; his capstone project on intellectual disabilities and sexuality was awarded the Helen Rehr Award for Excellence in Practice-Research.

D1593280

"Triska's short book immerses readers in the sexual struggles of those with recognized intellectual disabilities. In providing us with a treasure trove of information, guidance, resources, and hope to deal with their challenges, the author is convincing readers that this population's sexual identity and sexual behavioral needs should not be ignored. Trust this able educator's experience, and your ability to help these people and their families will surely expand."

Stephen B. Levine, MD, editor of the Handbook of
Clinical Sexuality for Mental Health Professionals

"This important book challenges agency staff to view sexuality holistically and offers practical ideas for supporting individuals with intellectual disabilities at all organizational levels. Triska updates us on the research related to rarely addressed topics (e.g. parenting, supporting LGBTQ individuals, consent, and offenders) and helps us figure out how to translate that into evidenced-based practice. This is a great resource for professionals supporting a new generation of individuals with intellectual disabilities."

Terri Couwenhoven MS, AASECT sex educator and author

"Sexuality and Intellectual Disabilities is a comprehensive, clear, and accessible guide to addressing sexuality and intellectual disabilities at the individual, organizational, and policy level. Numerous engaging case examples bring topics to life, challenging the reader to examine their current practice and more proactively address sexuality content. The book thoughtfully unpacks critical concepts of consent and privacy and does a particularly good job addressing LGBTQ inclusivity."

SJ Dodd, MSW, MSEd, PhD, Director, Silberman
Center for Sexuality and Gender, Associate Professor,
Silberman School of Social Work at Hunter College, CUNY

Sexuality and Intellectual Disabilities

A Guide for Professionals

Andrew Maxwell Triska

Routledge
Taylor & Francis Group

NEW YORK AND LONDON

First published 2018
by Routledge
711 Third Avenue, New York, NY 10017

and by Routledge
2 Park Square, Milton Park, Abingdon, Oxon, OX14 4RN

*Routledge is an imprint of the Taylor & Francis Group,
an informa business*

Library of Congress Cataloging-in-Publication Data
Names: Triska, Andrew, author.
Title: Sexuality and intellectual disabilities : a guide for professionals /
    Andrew Triska.
Description: First Edition. | New York : Routledge, 2018. | Includes
    bibliographical references.
Identifiers: LCCN 2017058602 | ISBN 9781138231009 (hardcover :
    alk. paper) | ISBN 9781138231023 (pbk. : alk. paper) |
    ISBN 9781315316406 (e-book)
Subjects: LCSH: People with mental disabilities—Counseling of. |
    People with mental disabilities—Sexual behavior.
Classification: LCC HQ30.5 .T75 2018 | DDC 306.701/9—dc23
LC record available at https://lccn.loc.gov/2017058602

ISBN: 978-1-138-23100-9 (hbk)
ISBN: 978-1-138-23102-3 (pbk)
ISBN: 978-1-315-31640-6 (ebk)

Typeset in Palantino
by Apex CoVantage, LLC

Contents

Acknowledgments

I gratefully acknowledge the clients, families, and professionals I have worked with over my career whose experiences are woven into the fabric of this book. I appreciate the help of Dylan Kapit, a special education teacher with whom I served on a trans awareness panel who agreed to be interviewed about his teaching experiences, and Cerridwyn Donaldson, a friend who answered my questions about gender identity and disability. I appreciate the support and patience of the editors who have worked with me on this project: Elizabeth Graber, George Zimmar, and Nina Guttapalle. I am thankful for the support of my wife, Samantha Barbaro, without whom this book would not have been completed.

A Note on Gender Pronouns

This book uses the singular gender-neutral pronoun "they" to refer to unnamed individuals whose gender is unknown or unimportant for the purpose of the sentence. The use of such pronouns has historical precedent—indeed, it dates to the 14th century—and has fallen into favor in recent years as an alternative to gendered pronouns. It is used in this book both to avoid the clunky "his or her" and out of respect to people who do not identify wholly with either the male or the female gender.

A Note on Disability Terminology

In this book, the word "intellectual disability" is used as an admittedly imperfect shorthand for a large spectrum of conditions that have historically been referred to by various terms, including "developmental disability" (an umbrella term that also refers to disorders that do not always have social, intellectual, or emotional effects, such as cerebral palsy and epilepsy), "mental retardation" (which is no longer in use, but was generally used only to refer to lower general intelligence), and in the U.K., "learning disability" (which has a different and much narrower use in the United States). Though such disabilities by definition affect the brain in some way, not all of them affect general intelligence. Those people whose general intelligence is not affected by their disabilities are nonetheless included in this book because they are largely served by the same organizations and government agencies, and their ability to express their sexualities and gender identities are affected by the same issues—social, legal, and logistical—that impact people whose general intelligence is affected.

I have also chosen to use "identity-first" language rather than "person-first" language due to the stated preferences of disabled people. This means that phrases such as "autistic person" and "intellectually disabled person" will appear in the text rather than "person with autism" or "person with an intellectual disability." Following the lead of Deaf activists and other disabled self-advocacy movements, organizations such as the Autistic Self Advocacy Network have chosen to reject person-first language, stating that it portrays autism as a disease and implies that the referred person would be better off without it: "When we say 'person with autism,' we say that it is unfortunate and an accident that a person is Autistic, [affirming] that the person has value and worth, [but] that autism is entirely separate from what gives him or her value and worth" (Brown, n.d.). Some autism advocacy organizations officially disagree, but as organizations operated by disabled people (rather than families or professionals) largely accept identity-first language, it is this language that I have chosen to use.

Introduction

We do not need to be cured. We do not need charity. We need respect, equality and access.
A.J. Withers, queer/trans disability activist, in "Radical Model" (2014)

♦ A 25-year-old autistic client at your psychotherapy practice tells you that he wants his girlfriend to spend the
night at his house in the future but is worried about his
parents' reaction. What do you say to him?

♦ Two clients at your workplace, a day program for intellectually disabled adults, have been discovered having
sex in a bathroom stall. How does your organization
respond?

♦ At the OB/GYN clinic where you are a nurse practitioner,
you discover that your 16-year-old patient who has cerebral palsy is pregnant. What are your next steps?

These are a few of the many situations you might come across,
or may have already come across, in your work. If you provide
services in any way to intellectually disabled clients, you will
learn that dealing with sexuality is inescapable. You will also
learn something much more troubling: that it's surprisingly
common for staff at organizations that serve intellectually disabled people to ignore these issues altogether, or to deal with
them on a case-by-case basis, often with no consistency or oversight. Organization-wide policies on sexuality are not yet universal, and those that exist are rarely inclusive, many focusing only
on problem behaviors. Educational programs in healthcare and
mental health typically lack mandatory, comprehensive training
in sexuality and gender identity. Across healthcare and education disciplines, these crucial training topics have been ignored
or treated as optional.

This book will change your practice for the better. It will
enable you to take on issues of sexuality and gender identity

in your practice with confidence and skill, develop sexuality-related policies for your organization, provide sex education to your intellectually disabled clients, advocate for your clients to their caregivers and families, prevent sexual victimization, and build an atmosphere of inclusion in your practice. You will be able to use the therapeutic and educational tools you already possess to tackle even the most daunting clinical situations.

If this book has one overarching message, it is that sexuality cannot be separated from the rest of human existence. The segregation of sexual health has meant that sex therapy, sexual medicine, and sexuality education have emerged as separate disciplines from mainstream psychotherapy, medicine, and education, presumably leaving other professionals to avoid thinking about sexuality altogether. Your goal from this point forward must be to reunite these disciplines by incorporating sexuality work into your practice. If your clients are thinking and talking about sexuality, *you* must be thinking and talking about sexuality. Awkwardness and squeamishness will need to be set aside at the beginning of this journey. You will find that the more you talk and think about sexuality, the easier it becomes.

Though this book is primarily written for clinical professionals and educators who work with intellectually disabled clients, parents and family members may also find it useful. Direct care providers, paraprofessionals, milieu workers, and other mid-level professionals should find this book accessible without graduate-level education. Everyone in every practice area should be involved in this type of care. Clinical and educational skills will help, but almost anyone can use the skills in this book to bring high-quality sexuality-related care to their clients. We will call these skills **sexuality work**.

In the next section, we will look at what sexuality work entails and what professional roles you might take on.

What Is Sexuality Work?

Sexuality work involves meeting a client's needs related to sexuality. These needs may be concrete, such as medical care or a supply of condoms, or intangible, such as psychotherapy, education, and advocacy. Your training and resources will dictate what services you will be able to provide yourself and which ones will require the assistance of another professional or organization. Throughout this book, you will be encouraged to stop saying, "This isn't my problem" or "This isn't my area of expertise" and to start saying, "I can help my client with this!" or "I can make a referral to someone who can help!"

Your most common role may be that of an **educator**. When a sexual "problem" is identified, you will often be able to remedy the "problem" solely with education. Indeed, you may find that the "problem" was simply an uncomfortable question that other staff could not answer. Furthermore, clients are often not the only ones with educational needs related to sexuality. Your role as a **family educator** is equally important. You may be tasked with informing families and caregivers about sexuality issues, providing families with ways of reinforcing what is taught in the classroom or day program, and ensuring that clients' concrete needs related to sexuality are met.

If you appear knowledgeable about sexuality, you may also find yourself taking on a **staff education** role in your organization, even if your primary role has nothing to do with training. I have often seen this occur with LGBTQ staff, who are sometimes the only staff members with knowledge of LGBTQ subjects and are therefore called on to be the "experts" on anything from discrimination to gay culture. This might not be a problem if staff training is something you enjoy, but it will be important make sure that there are systems in place to build up other staff members' knowledge rather than allowing them to lean on your expertise every time the subject of sexuality comes up.

One important role you might fall into is one of an **advocate**. Clients who trust you may confide in you that a classmate is bullying them about their sexuality, a parent disagrees with their choice to use birth control, or a staff member is referring to them by the wrong pronouns. Simply allowing the client to vent will not be an option. You will need to take action on behalf of your client with those in authority and follow up to ensure that their concerns are being addressed. If you find yourself addressing the same concerns repeatedly, you may even choose to engage in **policy advocacy** in your larger organization or with local, state, and federal government agencies.

Clients may also have **concrete needs** related to sexuality that you may be called on to meet. If a client asks you where to find free condoms or STD testing, where will you look? Now may be the time to compile knowledge of local sexuality resources to ensure that you're not caught off-guard when your help is required. Local LGBTQ organizations and family planning organizations such as Planned Parenthood can be excellent resources, and the appendices list many of these for your information.

A Radical Approach

In order to begin doing this work, you will need a theoretical model of disability that explains *why* your clients experience difficulties expressing their sexuality and gender identity—in other words, why your work in this area is needed to begin with. (And no, you did not leave theory behind in grad school!) The **radical model** of disability was originally defined by A.J. Withers, a queer and trans disability activist whose series of zines titled *If I Can't Dance, Is It Still My Revolution?* popularized this framework and lent a voice to marginalized and excluded activists in radical politics. In Withers' words, the "tragedy of disability is not our minds and bodies but oppression, exclusion and marginalization" (Withers, 2014).

In Withers' model, the hardships of disability are seen to stem from external factors like poverty and stigma, and not from innate characteristics or deficiencies of disabled people. In contrast to disability writers who focus on independence, Withers sees *inter*dependence as normal and necessary. Writing in *Disability Politics & Theory* (emphasis mine), Withers states:

> Chances are, disabled or not, you don't grow all of your food. Chances are, you didn't build the car, bike, wheelchair, subway, shoes or bus that transports you. . . . The difference between the needs that many disabled people have and the needs of people who are not labeled as disabled

is that **non-disabled people have had their dependencies normalized**. The world has been built to accommodate certain needs and call the people who need those things independent, while other needs are considered exceptional. . . . We are all interdependent. This interdependence is not weakness; rather, it is part of our humanity.

(Withers, 2012)

This model creates a perfect jumping-off point for conducting sexuality work with intellectually disabled people. Take a look at the physical and social world around you. Unless you are disabled yourself, you will find that the structures of your world—the subway that takes you to your job, the aisles of your local supermarket, the computer systems you use at work, the bar you visit after work, the government agencies and nonprofits where important decisions are made—were built to accommodate you. Can you say the same for your clients? Are they invited to help make the laws and decisions that affect their lives? (I know of very few places where this is true). Is your public transportation network built for people with anxiety disorders, hearing impairment, or mobility issues? (Many of my own clients complain of inaccessible buses and subways, and accessible transportation is notoriously unreliable). Is it easy to participate in your local LGBTQ community if you have a disability? (If you frequent LGBTQ venues, imagine navigating your local gay nightclub in a wheelchair, with a visual impairment, or with the sensory issues often present in autistic people). Do TV shows depict people who look like your clients, and do these characters engage in romantic and sexual relationships? (With few exceptions, probably not).

Everywhere you look, the social and sexual landscape is designed around the needs of able people. Your role is to join your clients in bridging the gap between their needs and what the world has offered them so far. This book will teach you how to do this compassionately, competently, and confidently. Case studies at the end of each chapter drawn from composites of the author's and others' experiences will provide you with jumping-off points for individual reflection and group or classroom discussion.

1

Sex Education

A program from the U.K. educational channel Teachers TV (Wells, 2008) shows a scene that, to American eyes, may be startling: a group of young children in a special education classroom absorbed in a sex education lesson. An anatomically correct baby doll is passed between them. "Vagina," their teacher declares in a broad Nottingham accent, pointing to the doll. "That's called a vagina." Later, a group of teenage girls are shown discussing the difference between friends and romantic partners, and a group of boys role-play about what you should do if a stranger tries to go into the bathroom with you. This is the Shepherd School, a special education school in Nottingham, England, where students are taught about bodies and sexuality from the very beginning of their education. For intellectually typical people, says headteacher David Stewart,

> it's not what we have in school. It's what we learn from our friends, what we're able to read, what we saw on the television. If you can't read, if you can't distinguish what's being said on the television, if you don't have those opportunities to go for sleepovers and whatever—where is

your learning coming from? How important, therefore, it is that the schools provide that education.

(Wells, 2008)

Parents at the Nottingham school are given the opportunity to hear about what their children are learning at parent-teacher meetings, and Stewart finds that few object when they learn the content of the curriculum (Wells, 2008). The extent and thoroughness of the teaching methods shown in the half-hour program are revolutionary compared to what most adults remember about sex education, which may have been nothing more than a brief video in high school health class. (Information on accessing this half-hour video can be found in Appendix A).

Sex education represents one of the least understood topics in special education. Even well into the 21st century, sex education in the United States—for both intellectually disabled and non-disabled people—tends to be woefully inadequate and starts at a problematically late age. Speaking to a young special education teacher I met while serving on a gender identity panel confirmed much of what I'd discovered through the academic literature on the subject—that sexuality and gender education tends to be provided *re*actively rather than *pro*actively if it is provided at all. In other words, education on sexuality and gender identity tends to be provided only when a "problem" occurs or students ask questions. Often, and especially in lower grades, there is little or no information provided proactively, such as in a standard sexuality curriculum. This appears to be common—in fact, almost universal—among those who work with intellectually disabled people (Schaafsma, Kok, Stoffelen, & Curfs, 2014; Thompson et al., 2014).

However, as professionals, this provides us with an excellent opportunity to work for change in our practice settings. Sex education can be provided by a wide variety of professionals, from teachers to social workers to direct care staff, and can be a part of almost any life skills curriculum. It can be delivered either individually or in groups and can cost surprisingly little to implement as part of an existing program. In the following sections, you will learn about the sexual knowledge that your clients need, the various ways of providing it, and the ways in which you can engage families in the sex education process.

Sexuality Knowledge: What Do Intellectually Disabled People Need to Know?

Designing a sex education program means setting specific, measurable learning goals. What skills do you want your students to be able to harness outside the classroom? Out of many possible sexuality topics, which ones will be most useful to your population? What knowledge do children, adolescents, and adults need at minimum to function in daily life? What knowledge do your specific students or clients need that might *not* be covered in a sex education curriculum for non-special-needs students?

Advocates for Youth, a nonprofit dedicated to advancing reproductive and sexual health education, has published a set of guidelines on sex education curriculum content, the *National Sexuality Standards: Core Content and Skills, K-12*. These guidelines (Advocates for Youth, 2011) are drawn from current research on sexuality and sex education and were originally designed to address inconsistencies in sex education curricula. The content areas that the *Standards* suggest for a comprehensive sex education curriculum are **anatomy and physiology, puberty and adolescent development, identity** (which covers such topics as gender identity, gender expectations and stereotypes, and sexual orientation), **pregnancy and reproduction, sexually transmitted diseases and HIV, healthy relationships,** and **personal safety** (Advocates for Youth, 2011). The report is available for free online and includes a detailed breakdown of specific knowledge and skills by age and grade level.

The *Standards* are intended to provide a minimum standard for a K-12 sexuality education curriculum. There is no reason to believe that sex educators for young intellectually disabled people should teach any fewer topics or devote less attention to any particular topic. Furthermore, though the *Standards'* content areas are tailored to K-12 students, all of these topics are equally appropriate for adult learners—even the topic of puberty and adolescent development, which sex educators could use as a teaching opportunity to add to clients' existing knowledge about human development and address myths and misconceptions about human development that they may have learned earlier in life.

However, even given the *Standards'* universal applicability, there are other topics that a special education curriculum may need to emphasize more than a general education curriculum would or to teach in a different way. Based on current research in special needs sex education, educators should pay particular notice to these topics in the creation of a curriculum:

1. **Consent and safety.** Intellectually disabled people are more likely than the general population to be the victims of abuse. Your curriculum will need to pay specific attention to students' ability to recognize and report abuse. See Chapter 2 for more information on interventions specifically for abuse prevention.

2. **Sexual pleasure.** Studies show that intellectually disabled people—and women in particular—often do not associate sex with pleasure, feel that sex is "dirty" or prohibited, and associate sex with negative consequences (Bernert & Ogletree, 2012; Fitzgerald & Withers, 2011). Shame and fear may prevent your students or clients from enjoying solo or partnered sexuality, even if there are no obvious physical or logistical barriers. Because of this, your curriculum should include positive depictions of sexuality that focus on fun and enjoyment as their own goals, distinct from reproduction, marriage, and other concepts. It should also specifically address **female sexual pleasure** and **masturbation**.

3. **Public and private behavior.** While a general education curriculum assumes that all but the youngest children will learn appropriate behavior from their peers, a special education curriculum may need to reinforce social appropriateness at all ages and levels of ability. This is particularly important in light of the potential legal consequences of adults engaging in sexual behavior in public (see Chapter 6).

4. **LGBTQ identities.** There are often few opportunities for LGBTQ intellectually disabled people to explore their

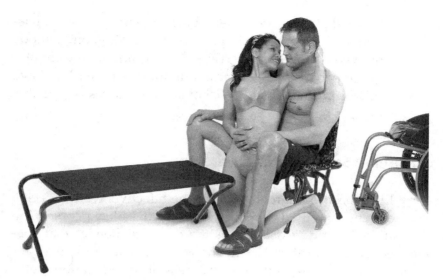

FIGURE 1.1 *The IntimateRider, An Article of Assistive Furniture for People with Spinal Injuries*

identities, find information about sexual orientation and gender identity, receive LGBTQ-specific healthcare services, and seek community with other LGBTQ people. While non-disabled people may find LGBTQ resources on the internet, in books, or through friends, intellectually disabled people may not be able to access these resources due to limits in their literacy, privacy, transportation, or finances. Professionals need to be proactive in bridging these knowledge gaps and connecting students to the larger LGBTQ community. A more comprehensive look at LGBTQ identities can be found in Chapter 6.

5. **Self-advocacy**. Studies of staff members who work with intellectually disabled people indicate that they are often underprepared to deal with sexuality issues due to lack of training and clear policy guidelines (Wilson & Frawley, 2016; Thompson et al., 2014; Rose et al., 2012). Students must be prepared to advocate for their sexual rights and know where to find help if their rights are not recognized.

6. **Physical barriers**. Intellectually disabled people disproportionately experience physical disabilities and medical

issues that may affect their ability to engage in sexual activity. Educators should provide information on methods of overcoming these barriers, such as adaptive technology for people with physical limitations who wish to have solo or partnered sex. A list of such resources is available in Appendix C.

Choosing a Sex Education Curriculum

Very little recent research exists on the effectiveness of specific sex education methods for intellectually disabled people. The few studies that do exist reveals the many challenges that special needs sex educators face in choosing a curriculum. In a 2014 review of 20 articles on the effectiveness of sex education methods aimed at intellectually disabled people, Schaafsma, Kok, Stoffelen, & Curfs (2014) note that most of the articles did not contain detailed methods, materials, and program goals. When there *were* stated goals, they tended to be overly broad and did not usually define exactly what types of sexual knowledge intellectually disabled people should have. The authors further note that evaluations of these programs' efficacy often relied on written assessments rather than other, more accessible methods, such as role-play or observation. The authors conclude that the most effective teaching methods involved "modeling, role-play, rehearsal, and practice skills" (Schaafsma, Kok, Stoffelen, & Curfs, 2014). This is in line with what we know about how to develop an accessible curriculum in any subject.

Assessing Sexual Knowledge

Assessment tools are important for both measuring students' knowledge of sexuality at the beginning of sex education and evaluating your program at its end. The most widely used sexual knowledge assessment tool for intellectually disabled people is the Assessment of Sexual Knowledge (ASK), which was developed in Melbourne, Australia in 2003. The ASK consists of both verbal questions and line drawings and is intended to be used in educational settings with children and adults. It is a comprehensive assessment tool, covering every topic recommended by the *Standards* with the exception of gender identity. The ASK has shown high test-retest and inter-rater reliability (Galea et al., 2004) and was reviewed by 15 professionals for validity during its development (Thompson et al., 2016). Most promisingly, you can use the ASK no matter what your role or level of education: students, paraprofessionals, and professionals alike can administer the ASK.

However, a 2016 study on how clinicians used the ASK in everyday practice raised concerns that this tool used language that was better suited to higher-functioning clients and not as understandable to lower-functioning clients (Thompson et al., 2016). Furthermore, its topics may need to be updated to reflect the social and technological changes of recent years, such as the internet and social media (Thompson et al., 2016), cyberbullying, LGBTQ identities, and asexuality. Nevertheless, a tool like the ASK may provide a useful starting point in designing a sex education curriculum that fits your clients' or students' needs.

Teaching Materials and Methods for an Accessible Curriculum

As mentioned above, the most effective teaching materials provide opportunities for role-play, rehearsal, and skill practice. They must also be understandable to the large portion of intellectually disabled people who lack literacy skills. This section will therefore focus on commercially available materials that are **visual**, providing instruction without the need for literacy, and **interactive**, engaging students in learning through games, stories, and social activities. The materials below are also generally considered appropriate for use by staff members who do not have formal training in sex education or the budget to hire a trained sex educator (which may be appropriate or necessary in some settings).

The widely-used **Circles** curriculum, first developed by special educator James Stanfield in the early 1980s, provides a visual blueprint for intellectually disabled students to understand social relationships and levels of intimacy. Students are encouraged to visualize their social relationships in terms of nested circles, with

FIGURE 1.2 *A Visual Relationships Curriculum for Intellectually Disabled Learners*

the inner circles filled with close family members and intimate partners and the outer ones with more distant relationships, such as coworkers and strangers. Educators help students categorize appropriate social behavior by level of intimacy, such as hugging for friends and handshakes for strangers. The program consists of an instructional video, a large wall graphic for the instructor, and smaller personal worksheets for students. Teaching is done visually using colorful graphics and pictures of people in students' social circles. The curriculum is used primarily to talk about appropriate social boundaries and abuse prevention. It does not contain detailed information about sexuality.

BodySense, a U.K.-based organization, has created three instructional dolls to assist in special needs sex education. Two of them, "Desmond" and "Daisy" (pictured below), are anatomically correct adult dolls with genitals and breasts. They are outfitted with clothing and underwear. Sitting versions of the models and a miniature wheelchair are available. These models are intended not only to teach students about the human body, but to model social interactions, grooming, and other essential skills.

According to the manufacturer, many schools incorporate these dolls into everyday school activities and use them during assemblies. The third model, "Wendy," consists of a 3D latex model of the female genitalia and with a removable panel that opens to reveal internal reproductive organs. This model is ideal for teaching about anatomy, hygiene, menstruation, reproduction, and masturbation.

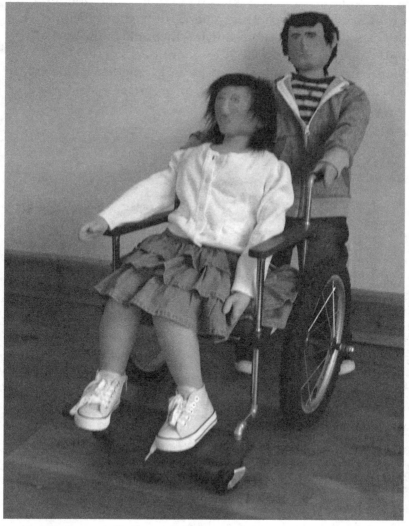

FIGURE 1.3 *Anatomically Correct Dolls from BodySense that Can Help Illustrate Sexuality Topics*

Things Ellie Likes and *Things Tom Likes* are two illustrated books about masturbation for intellectually disabled people that are both simple and frank. Other books in the series, *What's Happening to Tom/Ellie?* and *Tom/Ellie Needs to Go!*, address puberty and bathroom safety, respectively. The title characters in the books, though somewhat cute and cartoonish in appearance, appear to be teenagers or young adults.

CHANGE is a U.K.-based organization that provides short, easy-to-read illustrated booklets on sexuality and gender identity topics for purchase online. These publications include what may be the only accessible illustrated publication on LGBTQ people that includes transgender identities. There is also a series on parenting, another hard-to-find topic for intellectually disabled people. Other topics include pregnancy, masturbation, and abuse.

FIGURE 1.4 *An Illustrated Book on Masturbation*

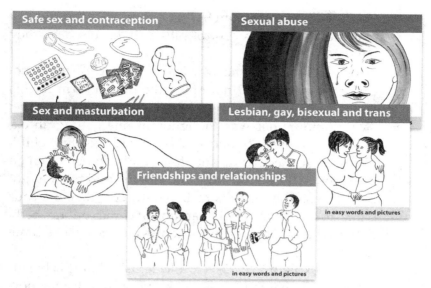

FIGURE 1.5 *Booklets on Pregnancy and Sexual Health Topics from U.K.-based Organization CHANGE*

In Appendix B, you will find more information on accessing all of the resources and techniques described here. In Chapter 2, you will find more information about sex education resources specifically designed for sexual abuse prevention.

Engaging With Families and Providing Family Education

The information you provide to families must be as clear and thorough as the information you provide to clients. Experienced practitioners know that it's unwise to assume that even an intellectually typical adult knows the basics about sexuality. A recent thread on social media and news site Reddit asked healthcare professionals for stories about things they've had to explain to adult patients, which included the following (edited for clarity):

◆ "I have had to inform a few male patients that the condom only goes on the shaft and should not be pulled down to include covering of the testicles."

- ◆ "Viagra does not prevent STDs or pregnancy."
- ◆ "People taking birth control pills only on the days they have sex."
- ◆ "I once had to use the word dick instead of penis because the patient did not know the proper term for his genitalia."
- ◆ "My grandmother was the ignorant one getting an explaining. She was 18 and in labour with her first child. The nurse looked her up and down and told her to put on the labor clothes. So she took off her top and bra and got on the bed. The nurse is really confused: 'Take off your pants, too.' 'Why? asked Grandma. It comes out my belly button, right?' 'No, darling, it comes out the way he came in.'"
- ◆ "Had to explain to a 27-year-old female that this bleeding she was having for a week every month was normal and why. She had two children, by the way." (/r/ AskReddit, n.d.)

In my own practice, I have heard similar misconceptions even from well-educated people—including healthcare professionals! This is unsurprising given the state of sex education in the U.S. over the last few decades. It is hard to blame the public for being misinformed about sex when families, schools, and popular culture make a great effort to stigmatize a perfectly healthy part of life. Given these constraints, though, this means that the instruction you provide to clients must be supported by information and counseling that you provide to their families.

However, this should not be taken to mean that family education should serve as a substitute for client education. In other words, it is important that sexuality information *first* be delivered to clients by a professional, not by a family member. Though parents and caregivers may be well-versed in sexuality topics, many are not, and it is difficult to know where the deficits lie. For this reason, family members should not be the client's primary source of sexual information. Never assume that asking a client's parents to teach him about condom use, for example, will result in this knowledge being conveyed to the client correctly and in plain, understandable language. Not only may the parents' information be inaccurate or outdated, but their misconceptions may be so deeply ingrained that it won't occur to them to check if what they learned from high school sex education or *Men's Health* was correct. Furthermore, due to awkwardness or simple inexperience, they may convey the information in a confusing way. Crucial information should be disseminated to clients by a professional who has the expertise to cover the topic accurately, use appropriate language, gauge the client's understanding, and provide regular follow-up to reinforce and build on what was learned. An analogy might prove useful in talking to parents about why this is important: just as a parent enlists the help of special educators to teach their child academic subjects, so might they need to allow an experienced professional to teach the client about sexual topics.

Consider putting together a packet of information or a newsletter for families about the week's lesson (see Toolbox: Family Newsletter). Encourage your clients to bring home worksheets and literature and discuss what they learned in class with their families. Bring up sex education topics during family conferences in the same way, and with the same ease, that you'd bring up academic or therapeutic topics.

Toolbox: Family Newsletter

Depending on the format of your class or group, a brief weekly newsletter may be helpful. A simple format might consist of two elements: *this is what we learned this week*, and *this is how you can reinforce it at home*. A collaborative tone is key. Parents will be much more receptive to your suggestions if they feel like part of the team. Here is a sample of what you might include in a newsletter:

Hello, parents and family of Mr. Madison's class! This week, we learned about personal space and consent. We talked about how our bodies belong to us and other people's bodies belong to them. We respect other people's bodies and ask them to respect ours. One of the ways we do this is by asking permission to touch, hug, or enter someone else's "space bubble." You can help reinforce these lessons at home by:

♦ Pointing out examples of personal space and consent in the media and in real life. How far away do the people on *Sesame Street* stand when they talk to each other? Is it a few inches? A few feet? Something in between? Why does Kristoff in *Frozen* ask Anna's permission to kiss her? Is it okay for her to say no? Grandma knows you sometimes don't like people to get too close to you, so she asks your permission before she hugs you. Why do you think she does that?

♦ Role-playing with your child. Pretend to be a friend, teacher, or stranger. What kinds of touching are okay? Is a hug okay? A kiss?

♦ Talking about body language. What do people do with their faces and bodies when they want to be left alone? What are some signs someone might not want to be touched or hugged? What are some no-touch ways of being friendly? A wave? A smile?

On our class web site, you can find some of the **[activity sheets, visual aids, games or whatever you'd like]** that we've used in class for your family to print and use at home. Next week, our class will be talking about hygiene and grooming. We look forward to continuing the conversation with you then!

Providing information to families may be complicated by the fact that sexuality is a value-laden topic. As a result, staff members often fear parents' negative reaction to sex education provided to their children (Schaafsma, Kok, Stoffelen, Doorn, & Curfs, 2014). Parents will invariably have questions—perhaps justifiably—about what, exactly, you are teaching. This holds true no matter how old these "children" are. Studies have found that parents of intellectually disabled adults tend to hold more conservative beliefs about sexuality than staff, though this may be an effect of their relative ages (Chou et al., 2016; Cuskelly & Bryde, 2004).

As the Shepherd School example demonstrates, though, transparency about the content and methods of your teaching may dispel parents' fears. Being guarded about your curriculum will not help you here. When parents see the word "sexuality," they may not be thinking about the full spectrum of what sex education involves. Seeing that your curriculum contains crucial information on topics like safety, hygiene, grooming, anatomy, privacy, and consent might help them understand the need for this type of education. Emphasize that sex education isn't just for people who are ready to have sex. Even young children and lower-functioning individuals can benefit from learning about their bodies and feelings and keeping themselves safe from harm.

Toolbox: Broaching the Subject

Bringing up sexuality topics with families can be intimidating, even embarrassing. This is doubly true if you have never been in a role that required you to do so. The following tips will help you connect with clients and their families in a way that makes you both comfortable:

- ◆ Ask the right questions. Use open-ended ("How is Cathy's relationship going?") rather than closed-ended ("Things are going okay with the boyfriend, right?") phrasing.
- ◆ Probe for more information if necessary. Try not to accept one-word answers such as "fine" or "good." You may need to build up trust and show your comfort with the topic before your client opens up, which could take a bit of patience.
- ◆ Consider attending a Sexual Attitudes Reassessment (SAR) workshop near you. SAR workshops are offered across the country by sex therapy training institutes and are

designed to get you in touch with your beliefs and feelings about sexuality in order to better serve your clients and overcome any embarrassment or fear you may have about sexual topics. These trainings also typically offer AASECT credits if you hope to pursue AASECT certification in sex therapy or sex education.

Competence

Being a sex educator also means confronting the fact that you yourself will need comprehensive, up-to-date sexuality education. The study of sexuality is a broad, multidisciplinary field with a constant stream of change. What you learned last year about HIV prevention or transgender terminology may not be accurate today. Training institutes in sexuality and sex education exist in nearly every major city and may count toward your profession's continuing education requirement. Even if you don't live near a major city, online classes, webinars, videos, and books can be your source of continuing education. Appendix A lists sites that offer sexuality information on a variety of topics.

Apply Your Skills With Case Study #1: Day Program

You are a direct support staff member at a day program for intellectually disabled young adults that aims to prepare them for the workforce. During a day trip to a state capitol, you notice that a male participant, Adam, makes several comments about a female staff member being his "girlfriend." This staff member looks uncomfortable, but the rest of the staff laugh it off and no one directly address the behavior with Adam. Later that afternoon, you overhear another participant, Georgette, asking a male participant, Roger, to hold hands with her, to which he agrees. Another staff member snaps at them that this is inappropriate. Both Georgette and Roger look embarrassed and avoid each other for the rest of the afternoon.

1. How could staff members have better responded to each of these situations, either in the moment or later on? How might you follow up with your manager after what you observed?
2. The staff member who scolded Georgette and Roger seemed to believe that their behavior was a problem. Do you agree? If a client's behavior *is* inappropriate for a particular setting (e.g. the workplace), how could staff talk to them about it without implying that their relationship itself was the problem? How would you use language that respects their adulthood during this conversation?
3. What kinds of educational interventions could the organization provide, either one-on-one or for all participants, to provide participants with information about relationships? How would you go about bringing this up with organizational leadership?

2

Consent and Victimization

In 2015, the *New York Times* (Engber, 2015) reported on an unusual criminal case in which a psychologist, Anna Stubblefield, was accused of sexually assaulting a nonverbal intellectually disabled client, referred to in legal documents as "D.J." Stubblefield apparently believed that D.J. was of normal intelligence and was engaging in a consensual romantic relationship with her. Stubblefield claimed that D.J. had communicated lengthy messages to her through "facilitated communication" (FC), a controversial method that purports to allow people without verbal skills to communicate by typing on a keyboard with a facilitator supporting their arm or hand. FC is widely considered a discredited communication method, as numerous studies have shown that the messages communicated by FC are generated by the facilitator, not the client. No studies have shown that FC users can reproduce messages if the facilitator does not know the content of these messages beforehand. In this case, no one other than Stubblefield was able to produce intelligible messages using FC with D.J. At the time of the offense, the state asserted, Stubblefield should have known that FC was an invalid communication method and that D.J.'s "communications" were not his own (Engber, 2015).

This case should make you think carefully about the way that policies around sexuality, and particularly sexual contact between staff and participants, are handled at your practice setting. First, we have a clinician deciding to engage in a sexual relationship with a client, which is unethical regardless of how intelligent or communicative the client is. Second, we have a client's sexual partner acting as that client's interpreter, a clear conflict of interest that professionals like Stubblefield know is unacceptable. Third, the client has "consented" using only FC, a questionable method of communication. Even we accept Stubblefield's idea that D.J. really *was* communicating, several breaches of ethics have obviously happened. Further complicating the story is the fact that Stubblefield, as a department chair at Rutgers, occupied a position of power over D.J. and his family and was in a position to practice without guidance or oversight.

What does this mean for you and your practice? If you work at one of the few organizations that offer excellent training and clear policies on these topics, perhaps nothing. However, if you work in one of the many settings that don't pay close attention to preventing sexual victimization, your organization may be opening its clients up to a tremendous amount of risk. A 2014 study of staff members at schools for children with developmental and non-developmental disabilities found that a little over half of perpetrators of sexual maltreatment were employees, and nearly one quarter of respondents reported that their practice setting "did nothing" in response to allegations of abuse (Caldas & Bensy, 2014). Even setting aside the obvious affront to human rights, not having training on preventing and reporting abuse has the potential to create an incredible amount of legal trouble for you and your organization.

Prevalence and Risk Factors

Research on sexual abuse victimization in intellectually disabled people is sparse, and most of it focuses on children and adolescents. Studies on this population point to a greater prevalence of sexual abuse than in the general population. A meta-analysis (Jones et al., 2012) found that an estimated 13.7% of people under age 18 with any type of disability are the victims of sexual violence, and while there was not enough data to estimate the prevalence of sexual abuse in the *intellectually* disabled population, the prevalence of all types of violence (physical or sexual) in the intellectually disabled population was estimated at 6.1%. One literature review (Stalker & McArthur, 2010) found that, among all disabled children, those with communication disorders, sensory impairments, learning disabilities, and behavioral disorders were at particular risk of sexual abuse. Balogh et al. (2001) found that 49% of intellectually disabled children admitted to an inpatient psychiatric unit over a five-year period were the victims of sexual abuse; 62% were adolescents and all but one were abused by males. A 2005 (McCormack et al.) study found that among intellectually disabled service users who had been sexually abused, the most common location of abuse was the family home, followed by day services and public places. In this study, more than half of perpetrators were other intellectually disabled people, while about one quarter were family members. The most common concern raisers were victims and families, not staff (McCormack et al., 2005).

Many aspects of your clients' lives contribute to their vulnerability to sexual abuse. On an individual level, intellectually disabled clients may face difficulty reporting abuse due to communication issues and may also have difficulty recognizing abuse when it occurs. On a family level, isolation—quite prevalent in families of disabled people—can get in the way of receiving support services after abuse is discovered (Miller & Brown, 2014) and may complicate efforts to prevent further instances of abuse. On an organizational level, lack of staff training and inadequate policies can lead to gaps in your ability to prevent abuse or to detect it when it happens. In the next section, you will learn how these risk factors can be mitigated in practice.

Client Interventions for Abuse Prevention

In the last chapter, we learned about general sex education and how to make your curriculum accessible. In this section, we will discuss two educational interventions specifically targeted for the prevention of sexual abuse. Other curricula exist, but these two are the most empirically validated of those currently in use and are able to fit the needs of a diverse set of clients, including those with limited literacy.

Sandy Wurtele, a psychologist and sex abuse prevention researcher, has authored the **Body Safety Training (BST) curriculum**, a ten-lesson training program designed for children ages 3–8 (Wurtele, 1990). Using a visual workbook, the program teaches both general safety skills (e.g. fire, traffic) and skills related to **recognizing, preventing, and disclosing sexual abuse**. It has been found to be effective in increasing both knowledge and safety skills in intellectually disabled children (Wurtele & Miller-Perrin, 1987; Wurtele & Owens, 1997). This program is ideal for a classroom setting with younger children, though it has also been successful with intellectually disabled adolescents (Lee & Tang, 1998). The program has several features that make it appealing for practitioners working with a general intellectually disabled audience. First, it is picture-based and does not rely on clients' reading skills. Though some text is present, it is designed to be read aloud by an instructor, not independently by clients. Second, it is not solely dedicated to the topic of sexual abuse. The material is presented alongside general safety material, emphasizing that sexual safety does not need to be taboo or divorced from everyday life. Third, the curriculum uses stories to reinforce material, which can be useful for students who do not learn well in a lecture format and need to be engaged with narratives. Finally, the curriculum includes a parent version, which can be used either by itself or as take-home reinforcement of the teacher version. Parents can be included as part of the educational process and home learning can supplement what students are taught in school.

The **Friendships and Dating Program** (FDP), developed at the University of Alaska Anchorage Center for Human Development, is a relationship curriculum for older adolescents and adults designed to prevent intimate partner violence. The core idea of the program is the idea that **safety training** by itself, though important, cannot provide enough protection from abuse

FIGURE 2.1 *The Body Safety Training Curriculum Handbook*

and must be accompanied by the **relationship skills** needed to engage in healthy, positive relationships. The content of the program involves both abuse prevention topics, such as personal safety and setting boundaries, and social skills topics, such as meeting people, planning social activities, and going on dates. The program is taught in 20 sessions over a 10-week period in small groups of 6–8 and heavily involves modeling and role-play, which, as noted in Chapter 2, are crucial elements of an accessible program. FDP has been shown both to decrease incidents of interpersonal violence and expand participants' social networks (Ward et al., 2013). Like the Body Safety Training curriculum, this curriculum emphasizes that sexual abuse prevention is not isolated from the rest of students' lives, but is highly influenced by students' ability to reinforce their personal boundaries and navigate difficult social situations.

In addition to these two programs, three other programs designed for intellectually typical youth have been identified as effective at preventing sexual violence as shown by a systematic review conducted by the Centers for Disease Control's Injury Center (Degue et al., 2014). These programs may be appropriate for students with a higher degree of written and verbal comprehension, as each curriculum involves reading, writing, and lecture components. The **Safe Dates** program is a school-based sexual violence prevention program for middle- and high-school students designed to challenge problematic dating norms and increase relationship skills. Students learn how to identify caring and abusive relationships, understand why people abuse, help others who are being abused, challenge gender stereotypes, handle their own anger, and prevent sexual assault. As the program is primarily based on discussion and role-play, intellectually disabled students may find it engaging and easy to follow along. The program also engages parents with brochures and letters that reinforce classroom learning.

The **Shifting Boundaries** program is both a classroom curriculum and school-wide intervention. The program's six-to-ten-week curriculum is similar to that of Safe Dates, with the addition of information about the consequences of perpetrating sexual violence and relevant state and federal laws. As part of the school-wide intervention, students create a "hot spots" map that identifies safe and unsafe places in school where sexual harassment and violence may be more likely to occur, and the school's administration can then use this information to enact greater security measures around these areas. The program also engages school personnel in revising policies about responding to sexual violence and harassment. The comprehensive nature of this program is appealing, as the burden of abuse prevention should not be placed solely on students. Engaging staff in school-wide interventions ensures that when students are told as part of an abuse prevention curriculum to report abuse, staff are up to date on relevant policies, and appropriate interventions are actually carried out.

The **RealConsent** program is a web-based series of interactive modules designed for college-aged men. While this program requires a high degree of reading comprehension and is not appropriate for students without these skills, it may be appropriate for students with greater academic skills who feel less comfortable in a large group setting and more comfortable learning independently, such as high-functioning autistic students. The program is designed to increase knowledge about consent and change participants' socially ingrained perceptions about rape, sex, gender roles, and alcohol by focusing on bystander behavior. Using interactive web-based activities and a TV-like serial drama, participants are asked to learn about sexually violent behaviors and commit to interrupting violence in progress by others. The program was found to be effective at both decreasing self-reported sexual violence perpetration and increasing bystander interventions in participants (Salazar et al., 2014).

For those who have already experienced abuse, **sexual abuse treatment** must be made available to combat its negative mental health effects and to provide support and comfort. Mansell et al. (1992) found that appropriate treatment was less often available for those whose disabilities are labeled severe or profound than for those with mild or moderate disabilities.[1] However, the authors note that traditional **individual and group therapy** are appropriate treatments for intellectually disabled people, and that these therapies can be easily adapted by a therapist willing to learn clients' communication styles and use both verbal and non-verbal (e.g. visual, role-play, modeling) techniques. Regarding group therapy, Mansell et al. cite Cruz et al.'s (1988) method of co-facilitating groups—with one therapist specializing in sexual abuse and another experienced with intellectual disabilities—as a promising technique.

Toolbox: Reflection Questions for Hiring and Training

If you are involved in hiring and training, this toolbox is for you. You hold the responsibility of choosing competent professionals and of readying them for very difficult jobs. This is especially challenging when training staff without prior experience in direct support, which is often the case at organizations that hire staff directly out of high school or college. Your budget might not allow you to hire experienced, credentialed professionals for every role, but any staff member at any level of practice can learn about sexual abuse prevention and follow policies appropriately. Ask yourself these questions about your organization:

◆ Are sexual abuse policies clearly communicated during staff training? If not, how do staff members learn them? Are they enforced? What happens when policy is not followed? Are staff members disciplined or retrained?

◆ What happens when abuse is reported? Who ultimately decides what happens? Is the decision largely in the hands of one person? Is there an investigation? If so, what does it look like? Is it conducted by staff close to the incident? Senior staff? External auditors?

◆ The highly-monitored housing, schooling, and work environments of your clients may work against you. Creating an environment in which participants can be assured of compassion and confidentiality if they report abuse will be nearly as important as preventing abuse. How do you protect clients' trust and privacy around sexual matters? What might get in the way of clients trusting your staff? Are some staff seen as more trustworthy or compassionate than others by clients? What do these staff do that others don't?

◆ How do you know what your staff knows about abuse prevention? What do you know about their attitudes about sexual abuse of clients or about client sexuality in general? Do you ask questions about these things in interviews?

Staff Training for Abuse Prevention

In "Sexual Abuse by Design: an Examination of the Issues in Learning Disability Services," McCarthy and Thompson (1996) enumerate many factors in disability services provision—some highly preventable—that encourage sexual abuse. In particular, the authors note that **staff attitudes** toward sexual abuse are not usually assessed at the outset of employment, nor are they usually evaluated later on. **Training** that could potentially change problematic attitudes is typically short and perfunctory, and no formal **evaluation** of such training is usually present. Finally, staff who make questionable decisions about sexual abuse prevention and response are often not subject to any level of **accountability**. The authors describe the case of a disabled man who had raped two women in his residence, which led to an investigation. Rather than removing him from the residence, a senior practitioner

> described [him] as 'having problems relating to people' and recommended that the man go on living there. When the man went on to rape a third woman in the home, nobody was held to account for their poor management of the situation.
>
> (McCarthy & Thompson, 1996)

In this situation, there were clearly no effective, consistently enforced **policies** on what to do when sexual abuse happens. Instead, this decision was left to the sole discretion of a senior staff member. Furthermore, organization leadership clearly did not discipline or remove this staff member after their actions directly led to a third incident of abuse. Clearly, there was no semblance of accountability at this organization, either for direct care staff or for management.

In "Sexual Abuse of Individuals with Disabilities: Prevention Strategies for Clinical Practice," McEachern (2012) concludes that **awareness** strategies need to be put in place, noting that staff and family members are often not aware of sexual abuse warning signs. The author also notes that parents should engage in **advocacy** for their children's right to receive sexual abuse prevention training if it is not already provided. This may provide an excellent opportunity for you as a staff member to provide **parent education** about their children's right to receive such training.

Training programs for staff have met with moderate success. Bowman et al. (2010) studied a group of 124 service providers from residential and day treatment settings. Participants were first given questionnaires to assess their knowledge and attitudes at the beginning of training. The Sexual Abuse Attitudes and Knowledge Questionnaire (SAAKQ) was developed specifically for this study to assess participants' knowledge and attitudes about sexuality and intellectual disabilities, and included such attitudinal questions as "Most people with developmental disabilities are 'oversexed' [have a high sex drive]" and such knowledge questions as "List five behavioral signs of sexual abuse." The Global Perceptions Scale (GPS), designed to measure general attitudes about intellectually disabled people, was also administered (Bowman et al., 2010). The workshop consisted of:

> (a) the definition of sexual abuse. . . (b) sexual abuse risk factors and patterns for people with developmental disabilities; (c) HIV and AIDS information; (d) how to identify physical and behavioral signs of sexual abuse; (e) employment setting factors that contribute to sexual abuse; (f) changing negative attitudes that contribute to abuse; (g) an overview of curricular and instructional packages for teaching AIDS education, sexuality education, and sexual abuse prevention; and (h) how to build safer environments.
>
> (Bowman et al., 2010)

At the end of the workshop, participants were tested again and were found to have experienced modest gains in both attitudes and knowledge. However, participants' attitudes toward intellectually disabled people *in general* did not significantly change. Nor was the change in participants' level of knowledge particularly encouraging: at the post-test, participants' scores were still low, at an average of 60% correct answers. Furthermore, perhaps due to the workshop being voluntary, participation was low, and participants were perhaps not representative of the staff as a whole (Bowman et al., 2010). It is unclear why staff attendance at the program was not mandatory, but given the common perception of sexuality-related material as a beneficial-but-not-necessary facet of training, this is unsurprising.

This study illustrates the difficulty of changing deeply ingrained staff attitudes about intellectually disabled people. Ideally, staff would be motivated to learn about preventing abuse because of a belief in the rights of those affected and a positive general attitude toward their clients. However, though sexual abuse prevention training programs for staff are relatively effective at adding to knowledge and changing attitudes toward sexuality *specifically* (see also Hogg, 2001 and Hames et al., 1996), attitudes toward intellectually disabled people in general are harder to change. Even people who choose to work with this population may not be aware of their own deeply ingrained beliefs. Furthermore, though training programs may somewhat increase staff members' knowledge about abuse prevention, this may not be effective enough to prevent abuse in practice, especially if staff is not engaged or invested in this training.

Recent research on staff attitudes toward intellectually disabled client sexuality reflects generally positive judgments, though misconceptions and prejudices must still be addressed. In one attitudinal study, Gilmore and Chambers (2010) found that staff members were less positive about clients as parents than about other aspects of sexuality, though both groups were positive about intellectually disabled sexuality in general. Males were viewed as having less control over their sexuality. Sexual freedom was seen as less desirable for intellectually disabled females (but not males) than their non-disabled counterparts. In another study, Meaney-Tavares and Gavidia-Payne (2012) found that staff attitudes toward client sexuality were generally positive; however, less than half of staff members received training in sexuality, the receipt of which had a positive effect on attitudes toward parenting and non-reproductive sexual behavior, such as homosexuality and masturbation. Level of staff education was not significantly related to attitudes, suggesting that organizations with master's- or Ph.D.-level staff should be just as mindful of staff attitudes as those with less credentialed staff. The causes of negative beliefs are not evident, though McKelvey et al. (1999) found that religiosity was a predictor of negative attitudes toward homosexuality, masturbation, premarital sex, and contraception.

These studies suggest several important factors in preventing abuse. First, abuse prevention must begin with hiring. It is much easier to assess staff for attitudes toward intellectually disabled people in general, and sexuality specifically, than it is to reshape their attitudes via training. Many times in my own practice, I have observed staff members with impeccable credentials and years of experience openly express contempt for their clients, disregard their wishes, or casually violate their confidentiality. It may be tempting to use experience as a proxy for good performance, but if you're in a position to hire, probe for problematic beliefs during the interview and don't skip calls to former supervisors. Second, even staff members with otherwise excellent performance may not possess a high level of knowledge about sexual abuse and may never have experienced any kind of sexual abuse prevention training, which may lead to overlooking obvious signs that a client may have been abused. There is no excuse not to have a formal training program in place and to refresh staff members' knowledge regularly. Third, policy development for sexual abuse prevention is absolutely essential. If your organization does not have an abuse prevention policy that is well-understood by organizational leadership, clearly communicated to all staff, and enforced consistently, it is time for you to advocate for one to be developed, or to develop one yourself if you are in a leadership role. In the next section, you will learn about the elements of effective organizational policies around sexual abuse.

Policy Development for Sexual Abuse Prevention

No abuse prevention curriculum, either for intellectually disabled people or the staff who serve them, can function without organization-wide policies to support it. Educational programs for abuse prevention tend to assume that when a client or student reports sexual abuse as instructed, the report will be met with swift action by the appropriate authorities and the organization as a whole will support those who come forward with accusations. This is where many organizations fail: clients and front-line staff *do* come forward when incidents happen, but the organization's leadership either does not know how to respond or does not follow their own policies. Abuse prevention requires an administration that is willing to spend the time required to develop specific, comprehensive, and individualized abuse prevention policies. Cookie-cutter policies adapted from other organizations may not address a specific organization's or site's vulnerabilities and may lull program leadership into a false sense of security, especially if they are out of touch with the concerns of front-line staff. Your policy development process cannot be a unilateral set of commands from above, but should be a dynamic process that incorporates feedback from staff and participants and takes the specifics of the work and client population into account.

The Centers for Disease Control publishes a comprehensive set of guidelines on developing organizational policies to prevent child sexual abuse in organizations that serve children (U.S. Department of Health and Human Services, 2007). As these guidelines focus on the unique vulnerabilities of people in care settings whose ability to prevent and report violence may be compromised, they can easily be adapted to policy development for intellectually disabled adolescents and adults as well. The following areas of policy development are based on the CDC's recommendations for suggested areas of policy development. Regardless of the mission of your organization or the type of clients it serves, these areas of policy development represent the minimum elements of an effective abuse prevention policy. Instructions for accessing a copy of the CDC's guidelines, which include information on where to find sample policies, can be found in Appendix A.

Your program's **environmental factors**, physical and otherwise, must be considered in policy development, and will vary depending on the specifics of your practice setting. Recall the "hot spot" map that students in the Shifting Boundaries program are encouraged to create and share with staff. What are the hot spots in your program? If you work in a school, perhaps a secluded hallway or backyard outside the range of security cameras is an area of potential danger. In a summer camp, rustic cabins may be sites where activity inside is largely unobserved. Think not only of physical structures of your program, but human factors as well. Is there a time of day when a single staff member is allowed to work with one or more participants unsupervised? Are groups of clients left alone for long periods of time during certain activities? Are certain types of practitioner given greater freedom to meet with participants alone or in a secluded location where abuse could occur? Are the rules more flexible for some staff members than others, or on days when the program is understaffed? Examples of policies to address these areas may include blanket rules about staff behavior (e.g. "never be alone with a client with the door shut") or rules about specific areas (e.g. "staff must not bring clients into the staff lounge"). Policies should also address the reasons such policies might be violated—for example, if the program is short-staffed and there is no one to provide "buddy system" support—and provide solutions, such as putting off a particular activity for another day or calling in staff from another area of the building. Building in "guardrails" like this can help reduce the disconnect between the organization's official policies and how staff actually behave from day to day.

Interaction guidelines can provide simple policy solutions for behavioral "hot spots." A common guideline is to prohibit such activities as hugging, kissing, giving gifts, and other types of intimate interactions between staff and clients. Though clients may solicit these interactions and may be disappointed that they are prohibited, there is a definite risk to allowing staff members to thin the physical and social boundaries between themselves and clients. Not only may clients not want such interactions, but they may also not feel comfortable saying no to them when they are offered. Depending on the setting, you may also consider setting rules on what interactions are appropriate between participants as well for the same reason, recognizing that participants can also be the perpetrators of unwanted contact. Your organization may also require rules that limit the type of support that staff can provide to clients. A day program for high-functioning clients, for example, may prohibit staff from assisting in toileting or hygiene tasks. However, beware of rules that segregate clients by gender or require same- or opposite-gender staff members for certain tasks, as these measures are not guaranteed to prevent abuse and come with other potential problems (see Toolbox: Fixing Problem Policies below).

Organizational guidelines on **staffing ratios**, such as rules that prohibit one-on-one meetings or set a rule for the number of staff that must be present in a given situation, are also an effective way to ensure monitoring of staff-to-client and client-to-client interactions. Address "hot spots" in which clients may be left in a group unsupervised for long periods of time—for example, at night on a field trip or in locker rooms during sports activities. As with environmental policies, though, be mindful of the reasons staff may bend the rules and plan accordingly. If situations that test staff members' dedication to following policy keep coming up again and again, you may be providing too little staffing, and even a reasonably ethical person might be tempted to take shortcuts. You cannot blame your staff for making poor choices in a situation you helped create. If there are routinely too few staff members to safely conduct a certain activity, something must change—either the level of staffing, the nature of the activity, or the way that staff are assigned. Never attempt to solve a problem with restrictive policies that you could solve with resources.

Behavioral monitoring is the day-to-day observation of the way staff and clients interact with themselves and each other. For direct-line staff, observation of clients may include being present in all client areas or circulating throughout client areas. For supervisors, observation of clients and staff members can include stationing oneself in or around the practice milieu, conducting random checks, monitoring security cameras, and maintaining staff ratios so that staff are never left alone with clients. Monitoring by supervisors should involve not only in-the-moment observation of staff by peers and supervisors, but regular formal supervision of staff members. These one-on-one meetings can provide an opportunity for staff to check in about their own behaviors and discuss potentially concerning behavior in their coworkers. Relationships between front-line staff and supervisors will matter here—would you report inappropriate behavior to a supervisor who played favorites, handed out punishments indiscriminately, or blamed the messenger? Staff at higher levels in an organization will need to be aware of the lines of communication between supervisors and front-line workers and ensure that staff feel that they can take their concerns to management. If you can't say this about your organization, or if you don't know, you're open to a tremendous amount of risk.

Response guidelines govern how staff members respond to inappropriate behaviors and accusations of abuse. Policies should dictate clear reporting structures for front-line staff (e.g. who gets the initial report, who is the backup) and what happens immediately after an allegation is made. When an accusation rises to the level that it must be communicated to local authorities, policies should emphasize that staff should not be in the position of investigating the truth of allegations or fact-finding before the incident is reported to law enforcement or child protective services. This is an area of policy that organizations should spend time developing with the assistance of an attorney who is familiar with local laws and the responsibilities of agencies to their clients.

Toolbox: Fixing Problem Policies

Too often, sexual abuse prevention is assumed to be furthered by policies that gender-segregate clients or prevent male and female staff and clients from working with each other. These outdated policies reinforce gender stereotypes and prevent clients from receiving a full spectrum of socialization and camaraderie. Furthermore, they do nothing to prevent abuse by same-gender staff members—in fact, they may make it easier for such abuse to go undetected. They may also fail to address the needs of LGBTQ clients, especially trans clients. Taking into account the original purpose of these rules, how can you modify them to address the potential of abuse, provide greater inclusion for LGBTQ clients, and curtail harmful gender stereotyping? The table below contains a few examples.

POLICY	PURPOSE	PROBLEM	SOLUTION
Only same-gender staff members may be present in the locker room	Preventing sexual abuse, maximizing client comfort	Same-gender staff members can also be abuse perpetrators, as can clients; some clients may be uncomfortable with nudity regardless of staff or client gender	Two same-gender staff members must be present in the locker room at all times, and private locker areas will be made available
A same-gender staff member must assist in toileting	Maximizing client comfort	Trans people and other clients may have different preferences	A staff member of the gender of the client's choice must assist in toileting
Group home staff may not hug or physically touch clients of the opposite sex	Preventing sexual abuse or unwanted physical contact	Promotes gender stereotypes, may not address trans/non-binary clients or staff, does not prevent abuse by same-gender staff	Staff may not hug clients, physical touching of clients should be limited to back pats and handshakes
Sex education shall be provided to day program participants in gender-segregated groups	Maximizing client comfort, ensuring relevant information provided	Excludes trans clients, prevents clients from receiving full spectrum of information	Sex education shall be provided to all clients together, and sex educator will also provide private counseling and education
Students' roommates in dorm rooms at 12-week college experience program must be of the same gender	Maximizing student comfort, preventing sexual assault	Not all students are straight or cisgender, not all assault perpetrators are opposite-gender, genders should not be needlessly segregated	Students may choose the gender or genders they are comfortable rooming with prior to start of program

Apply Your Skills With Case Study #2: Friends & Neighbors

You are the parent of an autistic ten-year-old son and the newly elected president of Friends & Neighbors, a local parent group that provides social events for the families of autistic children and adults. Though it has been in existence for five years, the group has not incorporated as a nonprofit and all of its events are staffed by volunteers and family members, with all funding coming from dues and small donations from local businesses. The group has no official policies or guidelines, so decisions tend to be made informally. During a planning meeting for an upcoming camping trip, you hear someone mention that Gary, one of the participants' fathers, "made everyone uncomfortable" at the group's annual holiday party last month, which you did not attend due to illness. The parents reporting the rumor differ in their accounts of what happened, with one parent saying that Gary made a sexual remark to teenage participant Marjorie, one saying that Gary merely made an off-color joke to no one in particular, and a third claiming that he made several sexual remarks and also briefly touched Marjorie's leg. Neither Marjorie nor her parents have said anything to the group's leadership about this and you are not sure that Marjorie's parents are aware of the incident. Your stomach sinks as you realize that Gary has volunteered to staff the upcoming camping trip and that Marjorie and other young girls will be attending.

1. What would your immediate response be? Would you investigate first? Inform Marjorie's parents? Talk to Gary? Call the police? Something else?
2. What rights does Marjorie have in this situation? Her parents? What about Gary?
3. Would your response change if the perpetrator was a participant rather than a parent? If so, how?
4. Regardless of the outcome in this case, what group-wide policies could be put in place to prevent sexual abuse in the future? Think not only of this specific incident, but of possible incidents in the future. Remember that parents,

volunteers, and participants may be either potential perpetrators or victims.

5. If you decide to implement abuse prevention policies,
how will you enforce them, keeping in mind the informal nature of the organization? How would these policies
be communicated to parents and volunteers? How could
you encourage participants to join you in helping develop
these policies? What kind of resistance might you meet,
and how might you overcome it?

Note

1 These labels are no longer widely used, as they are largely based on I.Q.
scores and do not reflect the many dimensions of intellectual disability.

3

Sexual Expression and Relationships

Writing in *The Handbook of Clinical Sexuality*, Deborah Richards and J. Paul Fedoroff (2016) tell the story of "Sam," who is one day discovered having a sexual encounter in a stairwell with one of the other men at his residence while a third resident looks on. The residence asks an outside agency that specializes in sexuality issues to perform an emergency assessment, and clinicians arrive at the residence and interview both clients and staff. They discover that all three of the men consented to the act, so they turn their attentions to the front-line staff and administration. They quickly find out that sexual activity of any kind is prohibited in the residence, that homosexuality is specifically frowned upon, that residents have no access to sex education of any kind, and that little privacy is available to residents. The matter seems simple—the residents erred only in engaging in sex in a public area, and it could be easily argued that they had no better options. The organization, however, has erred greatly in treating client sexuality as an offense rather than a fact of life. As the authors drily note, "a policy simply forbidding sex is as ineffective for people with [intellectual disabilities] as it is for the general population."

Any experienced clinician will tell you similar stories. In one special needs summer camp where I worked, a same-sex couple (who, outside the camp, lived in the same residence) were encouraged to use the term "sister" rather than "girlfriend" to avoid making others uncomfortable. In the meantime, heterosexual campers—some of whom had boyfriends, girlfriends, and children—spoke freely about their romantic relationships. How, then, to go about fixing broken policies that penalize normal, natural behavior, and which seem to be so culturally ingrained as to defy simple solutions? And how to align everyday practice with policy?

Who Gets to Have a Relationship?

If you are not disabled, you have probably gone through your adult life with the expectation that having a romantic relationship—or, at least, having the choice of whether to have a relationship—was a given. From the civil rights-era legal challenges to anti-miscegenation laws to recent court battles on same-sex marriage, the ability of consenting adults to make their own choices about sex and relationships has been recognized as a fundamental human right. There is, however, a pervasive double standard for intellectually and physically disabled people, whose sexual and emotional needs are often seen as unimportant or inconvenient. To quote Mat Fraser, a musician, performance artist, and outspoken advocate of physically disabled performers who has appeared on *American Horror Story*, "When you are disabled the two things people think you can't do are fight and have sex . . . so I've got a black belt and I'm really good at shagging. The physical pleasures in life are really important to me."

Historically, intellectually disabled people have been seen as either childlike and asexual, totally lacking in sexual desire and incapable of engaging in relationships, or as hypersexual, presenting a constant danger to the public with their uncontrollable sexual behavior. This can often be expressed in subtle ways. Disability scholar Claire Tregaskis (2004) recounts a time that she observed a women-only exercise session at a leisure center, which was normally closed off to men at this time. However, an exercise group for both male and female disabled people were allowed to use the facility at the same time and there was no objection to this—highlighting what seemed to Tregaskis to be a view of disabled people as asexual or "harmless." This impression was reinforced by a later conversation with a leisure center staff member who referred to an intellectually disabled man who had been aggressively asking the author on a date as "a lad." Moments later, reminded by Tregaskis that the man was in his thirties, the staff member shuddered and said that the thought "made her sick," seemingly shifting her view of him from that of an innocent to that of a predator (Tregaskis, 2004).

Even today, out of an abundance of caution, many professionals who work with intellectually disabled people will find any excuse to say "no" to their clients who dare to want sexual relationships with others, even those who are otherwise autonomous and capable of consent. The default, so to speak, is *not* to have a romantic relationship. It is regrettable that these professionals forget that their clients share the same passions and frustrations as everyone else and have only one life from which to extract as much fulfillment as possible. This chapter will outline the issues you may encounter in your practice and provide solutions to thorny issues of autonomy, authority, and human rights.

Privacy and Dignity

If one blanket statement can be made about intellectually disabled people, it is that they are highly likely to be more heavily monitored than intellectually typical people, with higher-functioning individuals given more privacy and lower-functioning ones surveilled more or less constantly. Growing up, this makes it more difficult to engage in the kind of sexual and social exploration that typical young people do. As adults, they may find themselves wondering exactly when and where they're supposed to have romantic relationships given the constraints of their lives. Some of your clients may feel that they've missed out on a vital part of existence, even if they have otherwise fulfilling relationships with family and friends. One question invariably comes up when thinking about these issues: why does it have to be this way? Is a lack of privacy essential to the safety of intellectually disabled people? Chances are, when you reflect on a given client's situation, you will realize that more privacy and autonomy can be easily accomplished in the context of the client's current routine. Consider Sam's story above, for example. Would it be difficult or dangerous to ensure residents' privacy in their own rooms? Would anyone be harmed? These are not rhetorical questions—in many cases, safety concerns *should* be taken into account—but considering the residents' rights relative to the small potential harm is a good jumping-off point for any policy deliberation.

Informational privacy is another important concept to review in your agency's practices. Clients may rightfully complain that "everyone" knows their business or that staff gossip about them. Consider how information is shared between staff members. Do staff talk about client issues in front of other clients? Is sensitive information shared with clients' families without any thought or deliberation? Do staff members carelessly bring up topics with clients that they may not want to publicly discuss? Early in my career, I worked at a program at which clients were given the task of shredding old files. Needless to say, the clients who could decipher these records found plenty of interesting gossip within—at least, until it came to the staff's attention and the practice was stopped. This was obviously against agency policy, not to mention federal HIPAA rules, but this clearly did not deter staff from taking this shortcut. The lesson? Focus not only on official policy, but on informal, everyday practices that can damage your clients' trust in you.

Toolbox: Basic Case Management Skills

As a professional who provides education or healthcare, you will probably be called upon to provide some level of case management, even if it is not in your job description. This will likely be out of necessity—many schools, clinics, and programs do not provide social workers or case managers, and those that do may overload them with work, forcing you to call on your own resources to help your clients. You may be the only person at your work site with knowledge about sexuality resources. At its most basic level, case management is simply problem-solving with clients, referring them to needed resources, and following up to ensure that they were able to take advantage of them. You may already be doing some of these things without knowing it. The following are tips to bring case management skills to your existing practice:

◆ Internet skills are absolutely essential. Though case management is certainly not my primary job duty, I am always being asked for resources, and these resources almost always come to me from a simple Google search. Many resources can't be accessed any other way—the days of paper directories are long gone. Bookmark useful web sites you find or use a tool like Toby (www.gettoby.com/) to organize your resources around particular topics. You may also be asked to build a sexuality resource database specific to your client population. A simple list or spreadsheet can be built for free using Google Sites (www.sites.google.com/).

◆ If you find that a particular organization doesn't offer what you need, call them anyway and ask for a referral. For example, if the trans health clinic you found online doesn't provide group therapy, the staff will likely have been asked about this before and be knowledgeable about therapeutic resources in your area, or be able to connect you with people who can answer your questions. There is no harm in asking.

◆ Build a network of people you rely on for services for your clients. If you speak to an intake coordinator, get that person's name. If a staff member is particularly helpful, remember their extension.

◆ If a client or family member needs to make a phone call to access a particular resource, provide a script for engaging with the person who answers the phone. Don't just say, "Here's the number to the family planning clinic" and expect them to know exactly what to do. Instead, you might say, "Here's the number to Rebecca Ross, the intake coordinator. Call her before 5 and let her know that you need to schedule an intake appointment for the teen sexual health program. Make sure you have a pen to write down the time and date. You'll also need to have your insurance card handy."

♦ Don't automatically assume that your clients acted on the information that you gave them. Papers get lost and phone numbers get forgotten, so don't leave out the crucial last step of following up. Depending on their level of engagement and ability, they may need you to sit with them and help them to make needed phone calls or fill out forms.

The Sexual Rights of Intellectually Disabled People (Legal and Otherwise)

Mentions of the right to sexuality and sexual relationships can be found in a number of universal human rights declarations and resolutions, though such resolutions are often primarily targeted at protecting LGBTQ people, as with the Yogyakarta Principles, which chiefly address sexual orientation and gender identity (International Commission of Jurists, 2007). Some declarations of human rights may be reluctant to name the right to engage in actual acts of sex, as opposed to the right to claim a particular sexual identity or to receive reproductive healthcare. Nonetheless, the right to engage in a sexual relationship is implicit in other universally accepted rights, such as the right to privacy, the right to free association, and the right to security of the person. The International Women's Health Coalition has this to say on sexual rights as human rights:

> Sexual rights embrace certain human rights that are already recognized in national laws, international human rights documents, and other consensus documents.

They rest on the recognition that all individuals have the right—free of coercion, violence, and discrimination of any kind—to the highest attainable standard of sexual health; to pursue a satisfying, safe, and pleasurable sexual life; to have control over and decide freely, and with due regard for the rights of others, on matters related to their sexuality, reproduction, sexual orientation, bodily integrity, choice of partner, and gender identity; and to the services, education, and information, including comprehensive sexuality education, necessary to do so.

(International Women's Health Coalition, n.d.)

Similarly, the Sexual Rights Initiative, a coalition of organizations seeking to advance sexual rights worldwide, takes the position that sexual rights are inherent in other universally recognized human rights:

Human rights refer to every person's freedoms and entitlements to live in dignity. This requires an environment in which all persons can control and decide freely on matters related to their sexuality; are free from violence, coercion or intimidation in their sexual lives; have access to sexual and reproductive health care information, education and services; and are protected from discrimination based on the exercise of their sexuality. These conditions are known as human rights related to sexuality, or simply, sexual rights, and the government of every country in the world is required to respect, protect and fulfill these basic human rights.

(Sexual Rights Initiative, n.d.)

For the purposes of your practice, this means that you must engage with your clients with an uncompromising sense of their absolute right to engage in relationships to the fullest extent of their ability and understanding. However, this also means that advocating for your clients may at times be a struggle. After all, there would be no need for universal declarations of sexual rights if these rights weren't constantly being violated, sometimes unintentionally or with little thought. Your workplace may have outdated policies or staff who are uninterested in clients' rights—to sexuality or otherwise. Your clients may even be unaware of their own rights and believe themselves unfit to engage in relationships even if they want to. Advocating for your client's rights means aligning your organization's practices with universal human rights to the best of your abilities as well as bringing out your clients' internal sense of their own rights.

At least in the United States, the intricacies of legislation and case law may come into play in deciding whether intellectually disabled people have the legal right to sexual relationships. Clients who are under conservatorship may have special legal considerations. One landmark case, *Kortner v. Martise*, involved a woman who was intellectually typical, but was diagnosed with mental illness and whose mother had been appointed her conservator. The woman—Kendall Kortner, referred to as "Kendall" in proceedings—was said to have engaged in a BDSM[1] relationship with Craig Martise, a man she had met online. The defense maintained that all of their sexual activities had been consensual, but the plaintiff alleged that Kendall had not been capable of consenting to a sexual relationship. According to the plaintiff, Kendall's desire to engage in a sexual relationship did not only conflict with her mother's wishes, but with her own right to be free from sexual abuse and exploitation. The plaintiff maintained that it was

> improper for the trial court to allow the defendant to present evidence that Kendall consented to the sexual conduct between her and the defendant on the ground that Kendall was **legally unable to consent because she was a conserved person**.
>
> (*Kortner v. Martise*, 2014)

In other words, regardless of Kendall's actual consent to engage in sexual relations with Martise, the plaintiff's position was that *any* person with a conservator could not legally consent to *any* sexual relationship. In the plaintiff's view, it was irrelevant that Kendall was competent to make decisions in many other areas of her life, including living independently and managing other interpersonal relationships. However, the Connecticut Supreme Court ruled that

> the plaintiff [Kendall's mother and conservator] did not establish, or even allege, that her appointment as conservator of Kendall's person specifically included the duty to manage Kendall's interpersonal and/or romantic relationships. Indeed, as the trial court recognized, the evidence demonstrated that Kendall lived in her own apartment, spent unsupervised time there, and was able to make decisions about her household chores and carry on interpersonal relationships, including those on the computer. Instead, the plaintiff maintains that the fact that Kendall was a conserved person was sufficient by itself to demonstrate that she was unable to consent to sexual conduct. **We disagree.** A bright line rule on this issue, as suggested by the plaintiff, would be contrary to the clear legislative intent as exemplified by the statutory scheme. **It would further affect the civil liberties of all conserved persons.** Therefore, we conclude that the final determination of whether Kendall had the ability to consent to sexual conduct is a factual question that the jury must decide.
>
> (*Kortner v. Martise*, 2014)

The case was eventually decided in favor of the plaintiff, Kortner, who received a substantial financial sum. However, the reason for this ruling was not because people under conservatorship *in general* were determined not to be able to consent, but because this *specific* person was shown to be unable to consent at the time she agreed to engage in sexual activity. That is, the court affirmed that people under conservatorship had certain civil rights with respect to their ability to engage in sexual relationships and left the question of whether any particular individual can or cannot consent subject to a determination of that person's specific abilities. This is in harmony with the balance we as professionals seek to bring about between protecting our clients from sexual exploitation and affirming their right to self-determination in their personal relationships.

The case brought renewed attention to the sexual rights of people under conservatorship and of intellectually disabled and mentally ill people in general. News outlets and blogs nationwide reported on the case, with some pundits portraying Ms. Kortner as a vengeful mother who disapproved of her daughter's interest romantic relationship and interest in BDSM, and others asserting that Mr. Martise had taken advantage of Kendall in a way that would violate anyone's rights, mentally ill or not. Whatever the outcome of the suit, though, much of the news coverage stripped Kendall of agency and autonomy and depicted her as powerless. Sex writer Maggie McNeill (2011), writing in a post on her blog "The Honest Courtesan," expresses dismay at the way that intellectually disabled people are often portrayed in news articles about alleged violations of their sexual rights. Writing about a case in which an intellectually disabled woman was allegedly held captive and sexually abused by an intellectually typical couple, McNeill highlights the way that the subject of the article is portrayed as "mentally deficient" by the media and implied to be completely incapable of giving consent, though she is stated to have been emancipated at the age of 21 and to have lived independently. Regardless of the subject's actual consent or victimhood in this case, McNeill argues compellingly that erroneous beliefs about the capacity of disabled people and what she terms "anti-BDSM bias" colored the news reporting on the case and dehumanized the alleged victim. Articles about the case, McNeill notes, depicted sexual acts that some people engage in consensually—quite common BDSM practices, in fact—as clearly wrong and unlawful in every possible situation (McNeill, 2011). It is also worth noting that such coverage also tends to reflect a certain level of discomfort with relationships between intellectually disabled and non-disabled people, perhaps by those who fear abuse and exploitation by the non-disabled partner. This reflects the presumption that only an abuser would choose an intellectually disabled partner, and that intellectually disabled people cannot be abusers themselves. Full recognition of intellectually disabled people as sexual beings requires that we acknowledge that they, too, have the power to abuse and exploit, and that restricting their ability to engage in relationships with non-disabled people is both ineffective at preventing abuse and assumes erroneously that they have nothing to offer an intellectually typical partner.

Clearly, our urge to "protect" intellectually disabled people from having their rights violated can tip us in the direction of viewing them as helpless. We do not have to give up our concerns about sexual abuse to readjust the lens through which we view our intellectually disabled clients. Recognizing our clients' right to be free of coercion and exploitation should lead us toward, not away from, a view of our clients as whole beings with needs and desires as real as anyone else's. In fact, it is the failure to see disabled people as fully human, not the recognition of their status as sexual beings, that can lead to sexual abuse in the first place.

What can we take from this in our practice? The most important practical consideration that one can draw from these cases is that law and policy treats intellectually disabled people haphazardly, with laws varying from one jurisdiction to another and agency policies differing by vast amounts. In many jurisdictions, marriages by intellectually disabled people are void or voidable. Laws are sometimes written vaguely—for example, the California Penal Code states that sexual intercourse is considered rape when "a person is incapable, because of a mental disorder or developmental or physical disability, of giving legal consent, and this is known or reasonably should be known to the person committing the act" (California Penal Code § 261). The specifics are left up to individual courts, which can vary widely in their interpretations of the law. On an organizational level, agencies that serve intellectually disabled people often provide sexual consent determinations to their clients, and while this is a great improvement over agencies that prohibit sexual activity altogether or restrict it on a case-by-case basis, there is no widely standardized test for the ability to consent. Your agency will certainly want to consult with an attorney when drafting a sexuality policy, as the intricacies of local law and legal risk management will be beyond the abilities of a clinician or administrator. Your clients and their families may decide to retain their own legal counsel if they feel their needs aren't getting met—see Appendix C for legal resources.

Working With Families and Caregivers Around Relationship Issues

When intellectually disabled people live with their families, or when families are involved in their care, their decisions reverberate across the entire family system. Unlike staff members, who are typically much less emotionally invested in clients, your clients' family members may see themselves in many different roles that are integral to their identity: protector, caregiver, supporter, advisor, or rescuer. These roles might mesh with your client's wishes some of the time, but sooner or later, there is bound to be conflict, especially if these roles don't evolve with a client's increasing age and abilities. Romantic relationships bring up issues that are highly likely to cause disagreements. Traditionally, relationships have symbolized some degree of independence—and what if the family does not feel ready for your client to be independent? A relationship also means that an outside individual is brought, temporarily or permanently, into the family, which can come with a host of practical issues as well as cultural ones. Perhaps most controversially, relationships can also involve sexual encounters. What happens when your client feels ready to have sex, but the client's family still sees them as a child?

Now is the time to organize your intervention around the client's rights, though your tone with families should be gentle and encouraging rather than strident. Invoking empathy will be an effective tool. Ask clients' families to imagine the situation from the client's point of view or to remember their own youthful struggles with maturity and independence from their families. Encourage your clients to talk about the way the situation makes them feel (e.g. "I feel angry because I'm not allowed to go out at night") rather than using accusations (e.g. "You never let me do anything"). See Toolbox: Basic Family Counseling Skills below for a primer on family counseling skills that professionals at any level can use.

There may need to be compromises, even when such decisions offend your values. Like intellectually typical people, intellectually disabled adults and adolescents who live with their families may find that they must ultimately abide by the rules of the family home. Restrictions that would be considered oppressive or even unlawful at a group residence are sadly common in many households where parents do not recognize their adult children's right to autonomy. This does not mean, however, that you cannot provide a safe haven for clients where their preferences are important and their confidences kept. Accepting that parents may make rules that clients consider unjust does not mean that you in your professional role must agree with those rules or attempt to force your client to abide by them.

Toolbox: Basic Family Counseling Skills

Experienced family therapists have plenty of techniques on hand to treat families in crisis and juggle complex relationship issues. But what if you aren't a family therapist, or even a therapist at all? Not to worry! You don't have to be a therapist to work more effectively with families in your existing practice. Those who work with clients' family members but are not family therapists—such as teachers, case managers, and direct support professionals—can apply these basic non-professional counseling skills to their work.

◆ **Listening skills** are among the most effective tools for establishing rapport with families.

   ◆ Anyone can practice **reflective listening**, which consists of rephrasing or summarizing someone's statement to show that you have heard and retained what they have said. Statements beginning with phrases like "I'm hearing that . . ." and "In other words

. . ." provide confirmation that you understand. While working with multiple family members, a reflective statement can provide a transition point to ask another family member for their perspective. Reflections can also clarify a point by eliminating digressions and tangents and focusing on the core message the speaker is trying to convey. Perhaps most helpful, you can reflect without necessarily agreeing with a statement. For example, even if you do not agree with your student's mother that the student is lazy, you can say, "I'm getting the sense that you've been worrying about the amount of progress he's made this year. I can see that it's been upsetting for you to see him fail his English class."

♦ **Active listening** is another trust-building tool. Simply assuming a forward posture and steady gaze can show families that you are actually interested in taking in what they are saying. Nodding and using small words of encouragement like "uh-huh" will prompt clients to continue. Importantly, do not appear to be eager to "jump in" or try to direct the conversation until all family members feel that they have been heard.

♦ **Discretion** means keeping your clients' confidences so that they feel comfortable trusting you. While HIPAA confidentiality laws may not apply to your particular role, talking to other family members (or, worse, people outside the organization) about problems they told you in confidence will quickly teach your clients that they cannot rely on your integrity.

♦ **Working with resistance** to change may be one of your most challenging tasks. Families might know that change is necessary to reach their goals, but also be afraid of disrupting the equilibrium they've achieved. The clinicians who created motivational interviewing, a therapeutic approach used in a variety of treatment settings to create behavioral change, call this "rolling with resistance" (Miller & Rollnick, 1991). This technique involves avoiding the tendency to push back or argue against a family's resistance to change (e.g. "But don't you think that your son is old enough for a girlfriend?"). Instead, you can use reflective statements about the family's reasons for resisting change ("You're worried that your son is growing up too quickly") and about their ambivalence about the situation "You want him to be more independent, but you don't want to be too permissive"). This serves to demonstrate your understanding of their reluctance, but also to highlight the reasons they feel that change might be needed despite their fears. You can then mix in statements that emphasize each family member's control over their own behavior ("The choice is yours," "You're in charge of what you ultimately decide to do"). You might find that families become more open to problem-solving when their resistance is framed in this way.

◆ Practicing **cultural competence** is a part of every family worker's role. While you don't have to know everything about the family's culture, you must accept that you are unlikely to drastically change a family's deeply-held cultural beliefs about relationships and sexuality—and that this is certainly not your role. Asking open-ended questions about the family's beliefs and experiences and providing reflections will be much more effective than passing judgment. You can balance finding ways of recognizing the family's cultural strengths ("Your family's closeness gives your children the support they need in a crisis") while also acknowledging that different family members may relate to these aspects of their culture differently ("How did you feel when you found out your relatives all knew about your new relationship?").

◆ Enforcing your own **boundaries** will make interactions safe for both you and the client. Some families may experience confusion about your role, and might feel more comfortable relating to you as a member of the family rather than a professional. They may even invite you to family meals or attempt to give you gifts. You will not be helping families by accepting these boundary violations as part of your relationship, as tempting as it might be to take this shortcut to their trust. Clarify your role at the beginning of your work, and reinforce it by making a point to practice graciously turning down social invitations or pushing back against unwanted physical contact whenever it happens. Even if this is uncomfortable at first, and it will eventually become a seamless part of your family work toolbox.

◆ You may need to apply **judgment** to decide whether a particular problem is more appropriate for a therapist, psychiatrist, or psychologist to handle. Family problems that might require intervention by a mental health clinician include complex or long-term conflicts, issues that may stem from mental illness or drug abuse, and problems that seriously affect functioning. You may be uncomfortable telling families that they need the help of a trained clinician, especially if they (or you) come from a culture that stigmatizes mental health treatment. However, your professional experience likely means that you have at least a few examples of successful family therapy to share with clients. Note that situations where you suspect abuse or mistreatment should be reported to the relevant authorities before any referral is made.

Marriage and Recognition of Relationships

Writing for the *Touro Law Review*, Marissa Debellis transcribes a brief interview with Amanda, a young woman with Down syndrome who is engaged to be married to her boyfriend of three years. Their dialogue succinctly touches on all the elements that make marriage a rational step for the couple—for practical reasons as well as emotional ones:

Q: Why do you want to get married?

A: We love each other. That's why. I want to get married, and live with him, and I'll be there for him, and he'll be there for me.

Q: What do you think it means to be married?

A: To be in love and complete.

Q: What do you think your life will be like after you are married?

A: I want to live on my own. I want to move on, get my own life with [him, he is] my partner in life. He'll be there for me, no matter what. (DeBellis, 2012)

This conversation occurs in the context of DeBellis' legal analysis of the challenges that might presented by the creation of a group home for intellectually disabled married couples, which does not currently exist in any form in the United States. The legal and funding challenges of providing publicly-funded housing and care for married couples are formidable, as one prominent case demonstrates. Writing in a column on the lifestyle site XoJane, journalist s.e. smith describes the case of married couple Paul Forziano and Hava Samuels in an article snarkily-but-accurately titled "Apparently, If You're Disabled, The State Can Decide Whether You're Allowed To Live With Your Spouse" (Smith, 2014). At the beginning of their engagement, the couple filed an Americans with Disabilities Act (ADA) suit against their group homes' administrators when the administrators declined to allow the couple to live together, citing the "unprecedented" nature of the request, which would be "fraught with difficulties" to fulfill (Diament, 2014). The residence where Hava lived, known as Maryhaven, stated that they did not believe she had the psychological capacity to be married, and even declined offer Samuels basic sex education. Neither Maryhaven nor Paul's group home agency, the Independent Group Home Living Program, were willing to work with each other on a solution (Smith, 2014). For now, their story has a happy ending, as another organization offered them alternative housing where they could live together in a supported one-bedroom apartment (Diament, 2014). Despite the couple's success at finding a suitable living situation, their parents continued to press forward with the lawsuit, explaining, "Life is uncertain. Who knows what could happen. While Paul and Hava living together as a married couple seems like the ultimate goal, this is so much more than that. . . . Now I don't know if the court is going to realize what this is all about, or what the judge might say" (Pinciaro, 2013a). In 2014, a federal judge ultimately ruled against the couple, writing that the "alleged discrimination is based not on Paul and Hava's disabilities, but rather on their status as a married couple," a status unprotected by the ADA (Diament, 2014).

Despite the couple's happiness in their new one-bedroom apartment—another article portrays them happily playing "Hava Nagila" and serving snacks at their housewarming party (Pinciaro, 2013b)—the ruling proved that the couple's and parents' fears were well-substantiated. After all, the organization that agreed to house them together could change its mind or go out of business in the future, and Paul and Hava would then have no legal protections against being separated once more. Though the case is currently under appeal, disability rights activists rightly fear that the outcome could have unsettling implications for the rights of intellectually disabled people to live with their spouses. What good is marriage, the case implies, if the rights that come with it are not available to you? How can you be married in any real sense if your relationship only continues at the whims of the organizations that provide you with services? These situations happen surprisingly often. Writing in *Sexuality and Relationships in the Lives of People with Intellectual Disabilities*, Sue Ledger (Ledger et al., 2014) recounts:

> A woman I have known for a long time recently met a man she really liked through a local music group. When she asked the staff if they could help her arrange to meet him again they said that as he was supported by a different service it would be complicated. Her support team are generally very helpful but this situation highlights how service-based systems can present barriers that staff find hard to navigate.
>
> (Ledger et al., 2014)

Both the story of Paul and Hava and this one are stark reminders that when you depend on a system of social services for your basic needs, and when that system does not consider your right to relationships a "basic need," you may find that your life has the potential to change drastically with the stroke of a pen.

Even if you are uneasy with the idea of marriage as an institution—perhaps feeling that it carries undue cultural weight, marginalizes unmarried people, or contributes to problematic gender dynamics—a marriage contract is undeniably beneficial purely in a legal sense. Paul and Hava's ADA suit would not have gone forward without one. Furthermore, from a social perspective, many disabled people are tired of seeing the world of marriage and family as off-limits to them and are loath to accept an alternative type of recognition when the formality of marriage is available to them. Though there is currently little research on whether intellectually disabled adults who marry are happier than those who choose to recognize their relationships in other ways, it is clear that many intellectually disabled people place high importance on marriage as a symbol of a happy life.

Non-Mainstream Behaviors, Identities, and Preferences

Above, we touched on the idea of bias against sexual behavior that is considered unusual in one's culture, such as BDSM. These interests are variously referred to by professionals as fetishes, fixations, interests, or kinks. (I prefer the term "kinks," as it is as free of stigma as it is possible to get when talking about these subjects, but still highlights the difference between these behaviors and more socially accepted ones—crucial when we talk about things like stigma and prejudice). Historically, atypical sexual behaviors have been pathologized by medical and psychiatric professionals even when they do not cause harm or are enjoyable and fulfilling to individuals that practice them. Furthermore, at least in the United States, our definitions of "normal" are heavily slanted toward Western norms. A fixation on female breasts, for example, is largely a Western phenomenon, yet you will only hear anthropologists use the term "breast fetishism," and it is not present in any psychiatric diagnostic manual. The DSM-V still retains such diagnoses as paraphilia and sadomasochism, though such behaviors must cause harm or distress to meet the manual's full diagnostic criteria.

Disabled sexuality is already in danger of being pathologized—this chapter has plenty of examples of how difficult it is for disabled people to be recognized as a competent sexual decision-makers—and an interest in non-mainstream sexuality further complicates matters. Even those who are more accepting of unusual sexual interests in non-disabled people may feel that intellectually disabled people are unable to consent to activities that sound too "extreme." Exaggerated fears of the danger posed by these behaviors may lead to shaming and punishment. This means that you may have to do a certain amount of education and advocacy in relation to your clients whose right to fulfill their kinks is in question.

Certain sexual behaviors and identities may be more common in intellectually disabled people. Though there is little research in this area, clinicians should be aware of these phenomena, both to lend support and understanding to clients with such behaviors and to provide context to other clinicians who might be confused or surprised by them. Educational resources for professionals about these issues are provided in Appendix A.

There is some evidence to suggest that autistic people appear more likely to become involved in the "furry" subculture, defined as an appreciation for anthropomorphic animals (not always but often sexual) that commonly involves sharing drawings via the internet, engaging in text-based role-playing, and dressing as an anthropomorphic animal character at conventions and meetups. A survey of 820 attendees of Anthrocon, the world's largest furry convention, found that 4% had been diagnosed with Asperger syndrome (Plante et al., 2013). This subculture has been greatly popularized on the internet in the last two decades and there are now thousands of online forums, imageboards, and discussion groups devoted to the furry fandom, with many furries considering furry culture an important aspect of their identities.

Many autistic people find fulfillment and acceptance in these communities, and the online nature of many furry interactions means that highly developed face-to-face social skills aren't required to join in. Others find that wearing masks and "fursuits" (animal costumes similar to those worn by sports mascots) lessens social anxiety and allows them to be more outgoing than they normally would be. It is also possible that external factors, like bullying and social isolation, play a part in developing an interest in furry subculture. Craving acceptance and social support, some furry fandom members find the community a more welcoming place than the outside world. Writing in a popular online forum for furries, one autistic user articulates the following:

> As for being a furry, I have doubts that [autism] is the cause of my furriness. The credit for that goes to the jerks that were in my school making [me] want to be something other than completely human.
>
> (Furries with aspergers/autism, n.d.)

Another user who claims no formal autism diagnosis, but believes that they fit many of the criteria and may seek a formal diagnosis in the future, writes along similar lines:

> I wouldn't be the wolf I am today if I hadn't been mocked and teased for my voice, for my intelligence, and for other reasons I can't name at the moment. I had no trouble making friends in grade school, because there were other kids with my interest in fantasy and science fiction and video games, but lasting friendship? Most of my schoolyard friendships were just that—the minute I left the schoolyard, they barely existed.
>
> (Furries with aspergers/autism, n.d.)

Another sexual interest that may manifest itself in intellectually disabled people is an interest in diapers. Though the origins of a sexual interest in diapers are not well-studied, it is common for intellectually disabled people to be toilet trained later in life or to wear protective undergarments into adulthood, which may create a sexual interest around wetting, soiling, changing, and other toileting activities as well as an interest in wearing and using baby paraphernalia. One such individual is described in a case study (Cambridge, 2012) that details a psychoeducational intervention from a rights-based perspective, which appeared to increase his self-esteem and challenged his providers to think beyond the supposed risk of his behavior. There is no apparent physical risk to wearing adult diapers or using them sexually as long as no bodily wastes are in danger of coming into contact with one's eyes, nose, or mouth (i.e. the same protocols that are followed for people who are in physical need of adult garments). Thus, interventions should be focused on helping staff members understand the client and avoid stigmatizing the client's interest further.

Though there is currently no research evidence to suggest that an interest in BDSM is more common among intellectually disabled people, anecdotal evidence suggest that autistic people may be more likely to develop this interest (see Nagoski, 2014; also see comments on article). The actual practice of BDSM may present challenges to intellectually disabled people; it may be more difficult to practice in a setting with less privacy, such as an adult residence, and it may be difficult for your clients to access educational resources for its safe practice. As with other kinks mentioned in this section, though, it can be rewarding and fulfilling for participants, even beyond simple pleasure and enjoyment. Shahbaz and Chirinos (2017), in *Becoming a Kink-Aware Therapist*, suggest that BDSM scenes can be used as a container for mental health symptoms, such as depression and anxiety. These practices can help relieve stress and tension and provide a way for participants to act out difficult feelings and desires in a safe environment (Shahbaz & Chirinos, 2017). One example is described in Kaldera and Tashlin's (2014) *Broken Toys: Submissives with Intellectual Disabilities and Neurological Dysfunction*. Writing in the first person, "Emma," a 28-year-old autistic woman, describes her experiences in a consensual master/slave relationship:

> I find that I take a lot of words literally, so being in a relationship where someone else is in charge and helps set

clear social boundaries and rules for daily living helps me function at my best. Add in the fact that I like shock value and kinky spice to my life, and words like "Owner and property" make me giggle. They fit the weirdness of who I am. I like to live outside normal terms, and it works for me.

(Kaldera and Tashlin, 2014)

Emma's identity and relationship provide her with a means to embrace her "weirdness" and allow her to view her differences, disability-related and otherwise, in a positive light. These benefits clearly go far beyond sexuality—yet another example of the benefits that healthy sexuality can have on one's everyday life.

Apply Your Skills With Case Study #3: Roxanne and Victor

You are a family therapist working with the family of Roxanne Barber, a 26-year-old intellectually disabled woman who has cerebral palsy and who lives at home with her parents, Nick and Judy. Roxanne's parents sought family therapy your clinic to resolve conflicts that they have been having with Roxanne, who is desperate for more independence. Roxanne tells you that she met a young man named Victor Ramos in homeroom during her senior year of high school and that they became best friends almost immediately. They remained so for years after graduation, even after Roxanne's family moved to a different neighborhood further away. Two years ago, Roxanne and Victor's feelings for each other became romantic, and they began to consider themselves boyfriend and girlfriend. The Barber and Ramos families are well acquainted with each other and seem to have a positive attitude about Roxanne and Victor's relationship.

However, Roxanne complains to you that she never gets any time alone with Victor. When they are at Roxanne's house, Judy is always checking in on them and seems uncomfortable when they try to leave the door to Roxanne's room shut. Victor's parents mostly leave them alone and seem more comfortable with their relationship, but Victor shares a room with his younger brother, who always seems to be playing games on his computer when Roxanne is there. They would like to kiss or cuddle, but have not gone any further than holding hands out of fear of being interrupted. There are also practical considerations: Victor cannot use public transit on his own, and while Roxanne is able to, her parents discourage her from leaving home alone. Victor uses a wheelchair, while Roxanne uses crutches. Roxanne confides in an individual session with you that she and Victor eventually wants to have sex, but both are unsure of the physical logistics and Roxanne is afraid of what her family would think if they found out. When Roxanne's parents are in the room with you, they seem ambivalent about the idea of Roxanne being in a romantic relationship. Nick and Judy both express both the desire for Roxanne to make her own choices and the fear that she will become pregnant or be pressured to have sex before she is ready. However, out of embarrassment, they have not directly spoken to Roxanne about any of these issues—in fact, the conflicts over independence for which they sought therapy are unrelated to Roxanne's relationship with Victor.

1. Beliefs about the kinds of privacy adult children deserve in their parents' homes vary widely between cultures and families. For many families, extramarital sex and even dating may be prohibited by religious or other beliefs. Thinking about the families you have worked with in your career, what cultural beliefs have they harbored about privacy? Have those beliefs clashed with your own? Have they clashed with what you believe to be the rights of your clients? How did those clashes get resolved?

2. What kind of privacy and autonomy does Roxanne seem to be asking for? How does it conflict with her parent's wishes? Are there possible solutions that address both Roxanne's desire for independence *and* her parents' fears? How much weight do you give each of these things?

3. What kind of conversation might you like to facilitate between Roxanne, Nick, and Judy? What if Roxanne does not agree to such a conversation?

4. What other kinds of interventions might be helpful? Educational? Group-based?

Note

1 An abbreviation of unclear origin usually identified to encompass the words "bondage, discipline, domination, submission, sadism, and masochism." The term refers both to a large range of sexual practices—such as corporal punishment, rope bondage, or humiliation—and to the subculture as a whole, which has formed hundreds of local and online communities dedicated to sharing information and resources about BDSM.

4

Parenting

"[W]hen I was in middle school," writes Roseminda Nabehet in *Thought Catalog*,

> a girl on my basketball team made fun of the weird lady
> in the stands wearing bright make-up, rainbow toe socks,
> and roses in her hair. Her exact words were, "Oh my
> gawd look at her socks," coupled with a pointed index
> finger and grin on her face that said, "Come ridicule this
> person with me." . . . I straightened my back, looked the
> girl in the eye, and said, "That's my mother."
>
> (Nabehet, 2014)

In this piece, Nabehet writes movingly about her intellectually disabled mother, touching on her mother's enthusiasm for education ("[S]he bought a globe, had me spin it, and then learn about whatever country my finger landed on") and her financial management skills ("On a minimum-wage job my mom managed to save a good deal of money and pay a mortgage") as well as the author's own feelings about how others see intellectually disabled parents ("To finally fully answer that asshole that

I dated—no, I never had ice cream as a meal"). She does not omit the less idyllic aspects of her childhood, describing an incident in which a con man took financial advantage of her mother, eventually causing her to lose custody of Nabehet for a period of time (Nabehet, 2014).

Nabehet's account, in its honesty about the difficulties of parenting while disabled, raises the question of what skills are required to be a parent. If Nabehet's mother was, by her account, an excellent role model and caregiver, who is to say that other intellectually disabled parents can't do the same? Why does society instinctively judge parenting by intellectually disabled people to be fundamentally different from parenting by intellectually typical people? How can professionals begin to dig deeper into our assumptions about disabled parenting to better serve our clients who are parents?

Who Is Allowed to be a Parent?

Parenthood has long been a controversial right for disabled people, intellectually or otherwise. At the height of the eugenics movement, Oliver Wendell Holmes famously wrote in his majority opinion in *Buck v. Bell*—a 1927 case that culminated in a ruling that forcibly sterilizing intellectually disabled people was not unconstitutional—that "[t]hree generations of imbeciles are enough." This ruling set the stage for decades of compulsory sterilization of people deemed unfit to pass on their genes. In the ensuing years, tens of thousands of compulsory or coercive sterilizations would be performed as part of programs that disproportionately targeted people of color, the poor, and the incarcerated. Even after eugenics programs were dismantled in the United States in 1970s, intellectually disabled people continued to battle child welfare systems that failed to understand their families' needs.

A 2016 *New York Magazine* article (Miller, 2016) asks, "How Smart Do You Have to Be to Raise a Child?", touching on themes of human rights, inclusion, and the often impossible standards faced by disabled people. The article profiles Sara, a young woman with an intellectual disability whose purported lack of parenting skills caused state authorities to remove her daughter, Dana, from her care before she was even allowed to take Dana home from the hospital. Sara, who was diagnosed with an intellectual disability in childhood and whose ability was estimated in the borderline range of intellectual functioning, was an enthusiastic parent, but struggled with basic skills from the beginning. One morning, shortly after Dana's birth,

> two investigators from DCF appeared in Sara's room. One of them . . . asked Sara a bunch of questions. Who was the baby's father? Who planned to care for the child? Kim explained that Sara would be the mother—but that, as the grandmother, she would help. Then [a DCF investigator] asked Sara to show him that she could swaddle; she made an attempt, trying to wrap Dana snugly into a receiving blanket, but 'it wasn't good enough,' she remembers. 'I didn't do it right. He pushed me out of the way and said, "Let me see if I can do it," kind of joking about it. And they're like, "Oh, you can't do this." Like, very negative.
>
> (Miller, 2016)

Dana was removed from Sara's care and placed with a foster family, where she remained for two years. During that time, Sara was permitted only two visits per month of one hour each, always with a social worker present. She had little chance to bond with her child or to demonstrate parenting skills to any great degree. The burden of proof was on Sara to show that she was not a danger to her child. Child services workers noted that Dana's foster parents were skilled caregivers and had bonded with the child—the implication being that Dana was better off with *any* parents whose skills were greater than her biological mother's, even if her mother managed to become a competent parent (Miller, 2016).

Like many new parents, Sara was clumsy and uncomfortable with some parenting tasks, such as changing diapers. Unlike intellectually typical parents, though, Sara's deficits were assumed to stem from her disability rather than her lack of experience or simply being overwhelmed. The state's interventions focused less on building her ability to parent her child than on warding off any hint of risk, even hypothetical. As Sara's story illustrates, intellectually disabled people are expected to be not just good parents, but *great* parents—unlike typical parents, who are allowed to make mistakes and given the privacy to learn to parent. It is clear that Sara had fewer parenting skills than the experienced foster parents who had been caring for her child for the first two years of her life. However, this is clearly not sufficient reason for removal in itself. Providing an *adequate* environment for a child does not necessarily entail providing an *optimal* environment, and failure to do the latter should not be taken as a sign of incompetence unless it would be taken as such in a non-disabled parent. On this double standard, user "lizcoconnor" in the article's comment section writes:

> I was once one of those Foster Care Reviewers that Miller references here. I frequently found myself hoping that no day care teacher or neighbor would develop suspicions about me, because if the state investigated they would indeed find outlets without covers, missed doctors' appointments, bruises I couldn't remember the cause of, and myriad other sins which would be in the files as evidence that parents were unfit to care for kids.
> (in comments on Miller, 2016)

Fortunately, Sara and Dana's story has a relatively happy ending: after Dana had spent two years in foster care, Sara's parents, Kim and Sam, were named Dana's guardians, and Dana was allowed to live with her mother and grandparents (Miller, 2016). Not every family is lucky enough to have the legal and emotional support that Sara had. According to a report by the National Council on Disability (2012), "Rocking the Cradle," intellectually disabled parents are often the targets of child removal when there is no evidence that their children are being maltreated, reflecting a belief that these parents will never be able to provide a safe environment for their children, even with support. In other words, these parents are not only held to a stricter standard than other parents, but are automatically assumed to be incompetent until proven otherwise. The report goes on to note two additional factors that lead to removal: poverty and a higher frequency of contact with social services workers, who can often be a source of CPS referrals (National Council on Disability, 2012). It is debatable whether the second factor can be considered positive or negative. The rights of the child are certainly important, and having a trained professional monitoring a delicate parenting situation can be beneficial for a child's welfare. However, disabled parents may consider this an unwanted and unnecessary intrusion into their lives, and these professionals may be too quick to make a CPS referral when they would not in the case of a non-disabled parent. Furthermore, these "helpful" CPS referrals may cause disabled parents to refuse professional help when they need it, creating dangerous conditions when a quick intervention—a ten-minute tutorial on how to warm a bottle or create a safe sleep environment for a newborn—could have prevented the harm altogether.

Challenges of Intellectually Disabled Parenting

It is important to first note that not all problems experienced by intellectually disabled parents are caused by deficits in ability. As noted above, poverty can play a large (and often decisive) factor. The economic challenges of intellectually disabled parenting cannot be overstated. Intellectually disabled parents are much more likely than other parents not to work, or to work low-skill jobs that do not provide a living wage. They may struggle to keep their children healthy and safe even if they are otherwise competent caregivers. A parent who reuses diapers or waters down baby formula may not lack parenting skills, but rather funds. Furthermore, as noted above, parents may feel unsafe reaching out for help out of fear of their children being removed. Unfortunately, the child welfare system often penalizes poverty, and intellectually disabled parents might be too easily assumed to be incompetent even when the problem is solely financial. It is therefore important to be mindful of these limitations and to work with clients to ensure that a trusted person, such as a family member or case manager, is there to keep benefits active and direct clients to such resources as food pantries and diaper banks.

Other factors unrelated to parenting skills deficits can complicate parenting. In an online survey of autistic mothers—one of very few research projects to directly capture the experiences of intellectually disabled parents—such mothers were found to be more likely to feel isolated and unable to turn to others for parenting support, to find communicating with professionals difficult, to feel misunderstood by professionals, to worry about others judging their parenting skills, and to experience pre- or post-natal depression compared with neurotypical mothers (Pohl et al., 2016). Many of these roadblocks are purely structural and can't be easily remedied by a single clinician. A child welfare system that doesn't stigmatize disability would lower the stakes of speaking to doctors and teachers for autistic parents, and the wider availability of support for disabled people—for example, a public health initiative similar to the health visiting system in the United Kingdom—would help normalize the everyday problems of disabled parenting. Clearly, drastic political change would have to happen to make these services available in the United States. However, many of these stressors can be mitigated without cost by individual practitioners. If a disabled parent seems hesitant to speak to a professional or to reach out for support, it is likely a conditioned response. Simply taking the parent's preferences and beliefs about parenthood seriously may mean the difference between a parent who sees you as an ally and one who sees you as a critical authority figure.

Childcare skills, or the lack thereof, represent the single most complex factor in intellectually disabled parenting. There are no agreed-upon benchmarks for the skills required to be a minimally competent parent. The standard skills of parenthood are different in every culture and generation, often wildly. A talented mother at the turn of the century would be seen as monstrous today for giving her children soothing syrups (popular at the time, but often made with alcohol or cocaine) or for following popular medical advice to have as little physical contact with her newborn as possible. For most people, formal parenting training—apart from the rather expensive parent-and-child classes designed for the upper and middle social classes—tends to be culturally unacceptable, even when offered for free, and parents who attend parenting classes are often those who are forced to do so by family courts. Popular consensus seems to be that parenting skills are instinctive, that parents who do not automatically have them are deficient, and that reaching out for help with parenting from anyone but family and friends renders you pitiable or dangerous. This means that you must help your clients get past this stigma and affirm that the decision to seek help is both brave and self-aware. Not only is it unavoidable that some clients will need parenting skills training, such training can be of tremendous benefit even if some clients can get by without it.

Much of the discussion around parenting skills in intellectually disabled people centers on the concept of risk management: the idea that there is an acceptable level of danger in parenting, and that once this threshold is crossed, the state must either mitigate the risk or remove the child. However, just as there is no universal consensus on what parenting skills are necessary, there is similarly no agreement about what level of risk is tolerable, legally or otherwise. Laws differ greatly between jurisdictions on whether it is acceptable to refuse to vaccinate or use corporal punishment, for example, even though the risks of these parenting practices are well-understood. Furthermore, while some studies have shown poorer outcomes for children with intellectually disabled parents, such outcomes are not necessarily inevitable. One literature review found that when external factors are taken into account—such as pregnancy health risks, poverty, parents' negative experiences in childhood, stigma, and social isolation—child outcomes approach population norms (Collings & Llewellyn, 2012). Thus, even if we accept that certain levels of risk should result in child removal, it is not a given that having an intellectually disabled parent represents a high level of risk without actual evidence of neglect or abuse.

While it is difficult to arrive at a precise level of acceptable risk, it is possible to quantify the factors that can lead to greater negative outcomes—though these measures should obviously be used in a preventive rather than a punitive way. In one study on the relation-ship between cognition and neglectful parenting, Azar et al. (2012) propose that certain social and problem-solving skills—which the authors term social information processing (SIP) factors—play a major role in neglectful parenting. The three factors used in the SIP model are *unrealistic expectations about parenting* (e.g. the belief that a small child should be self-sufficient, or that a 13-year-old should take a parent's feelings into account to an unrealistic degree), *poor executive functioning* (e.g. difficulties in problem-solving, lack of complex decision-making skills), and *maladaptive appraisals* (e.g. attributing negative intent to children who misbehave, which can provoke disproportionate or unwarranted responses, such as ex-cessive punishment). These SIP factors, as measured with stan-dardized questionnaires, were found to be correlated with several measures of neglectful parenting: higher levels of physical neglect, lower home cleanliness, less stimulating home environments, less positive parent-child interactions, and maladaptive parent beliefs, such as the belief that being physically hurt toughens children up, or that injuries are the result of fate rather than controllable cir-cumstances (Azar, 2012).

Interestingly, IQ was *not* shown to be predictive of child ne-glect beyond that shown by SIP scores (Azar, 2012). The authors suggest that these SIP factors may be to blame for the correlation between intellectual disability and parental neglect (Azar, 2012). This means that while SIP problems may be higher in intellectu-ally disabled people, those with fewer SIP difficulties may prove to be perfectly adept parents. This also means that parenting skills interventions should focus not just on concrete skills like nutri-tion and safety, but on crucial social-cognitive skills. Think back to your own childhood caregivers, parental or otherwise. Other than their capacity to cook meals and clean bathrooms, were they responsive to your needs? Did they understand that children had different abilities than adults? Did they blame you for things that weren't your fault? Expect too much of you at too young an age? Misunderstand your motivations? Forget things that were import-ant to you? Deficits in these social-cognitive skills can lead to both emotional and physical neglect, even in parents with good con-crete skills such as cooking and safety. It is not enough to know how to cook a simple meal if a parent attributes a child's refusal of food as a personal insult, for example. Similarly, first aid skills help little if a parent does not understand that they are the one responsible for preventing injury in the first place.

What can we learn from this in practice? First, to be open to the idea that your core assumptions about parenting ability may be outdated. If you are wedded to the notion that intelligence and high functioning make a skilled parent, now may be the time to question these assumptions and delve deeper into the reasons for your clients' parenting successes and setbacks. It may be tempting to lump "cognitive skills" into one category, but SIP research seems to point to the idea that some of these skills influence parenting outcomes far more than others. Second, to acknowledge that beliefs and attitudes about parenting may play a much larger role in child outcomes than previously thought. This is especially concerning given that it is much more difficult to change attitudes than to teach concrete parenting skills. Childproofing a kitchen can be taught by a patient teacher to a willing student; helping a parent who attributes malice to a three-month-old infant might be a harder task.

In the next section, you will learn about methods of parenting skills instruction and the successes of different programs. Information on accessing these programs can be found in Appendix B.

Parenting Skills Training

Delivering childcare skills training to intellectually disabled people can happen in a wide variety of formats. Classroom learning, in-home training, peer support groups, and professionally-led groups can all be successful at conveying needed parenting information. Even self-learning can be effective; Feldman and Case (1999) found that a self-instruction course with pictures, simple explanations, and accompanying audiotapes was effective at teaching childcare and safety skills. Encouragingly, the program in the study resulted in participants retaining information more than six months after the course.

GIVING YOUR BABY A BOTTLE

15. Burp your baby again when she is finished.

   If there is formula leftover, throw it out. Germs can grow in warm formula.

16. You can talk, sing, and cuddle, during and after feeding.

   It is good for your baby to spend this time with you.

FIGURE 4.1 *An Illustration from the Step-by-Step Parenting Program Handbook*

There are currently two parenting training curricula that the California Evidence-Based Clearinghouse for Child Welfare has rated as having promising research evidence (California Evidence-Based Clearinghouse, 2015; California Evidence-Based Clearinghouse, 2016): the **Step-by-Step Parenting Program** and **Healthy & Safe**. The Step-by-Step Parenting Program was developed by Maurice

Feldman, a Canadian researcher who has studied intellectually disabled parenting extensively. Instruction is provided on weekly visits to the participant's home by bachelor's- or master's-level professionals who have taken a minimum of a one-day training course and who monitor skill acquisition through checklists in order to provide feedback. This instruction is supplemented by homework and reading assignments. Toward the end of the program, home visits gradually lessen in frequency as participants build natural supports. The second program, Healthy & Safe, is somewhat more limited in scope, focusing primarily on child safety. Modules include information on common home dangers (e.g. fire, sharp objects, clutter), recognizing signs of illness, visiting the doctor, performing everyday healthcare tasks (e.g. taking temperature), and handling life-threatening emergencies. Like the Step-By-Step program, the curriculum is administered by a parent educator one-on-one in the parent's home. It is self-paced and the parent can choose either to work through the entire curriculum or to focus on specific areas of need. Information on accessing both of these training curricula can be found in Appendix B.

Formal parenting programs for intellectually disabled parents offered by social services agencies typically extend not only learning opportunities, but concrete supports, therapeutic interventions, and case management. These programs recognize that skill training is only one component of successful parenting, and that regular check-ins with professionals can mitigate external factors that can interfere with family harmony. The following are the features common among parenting training programs.

Peer Support and Education

Close your eyes and think of the last time you saw an intellectually disabled parent on television or in a film. Chances are, if you can think of an example at all, you're picturing Sean Penn and the film you saw was Jessie Nelson's 2001 drama I Am Sam. Intellectually disabled parents lack role models, both in media and in real life. Your clients may not be able to point to anyone, real or fictional, who has actually accomplished what they are trying to do. A peer support group can solve this problem by connecting your clients to people who share their struggles and have found parenting solutions that mesh with their abilities through experience. Participants may also feel more relaxed among their peers and less likely to feel judged, as they might with a professional whom they may see as an authority figure or interloper.

Family Therapy

More often than not, multiple family members other than the intellectually disabled parent will be involved in the care of a child. These informal supports may be heavily involved in the day-to-day care of children, or may provide less frequent but still vital assistance in larger tasks like driving and bill payment. Conflicts can arise when intellectually disabled parents and their family members do not agree on parenting decisions, especially if they live together. Enmeshment and lack of boundaries between family members can make disabled parents feel as though they lack control over their lives and the lives of their children, and families may continue to see the disabled parent as a child even long after said parent becomes an adult. A family therapist—ideally one with experience working with intellectually disabled clients—can help the family recalibrate their view of the parent from incapable child to competent caregiver, even if the disabled parent is not fully or even mostly independent. Recall the quote from A.J. Withers in the introduction: "We are all interdependent. This interdependence is not weakness." A therapist with this mindset will be able to problem-solve in ways that do not involve the loss of the disabled parent's autonomy and decision-making power, no less when the parent is not the only one involved in the child's care.

In-Vivo Services

Classroom education can have the advantage of reaching a larger number of students at once, but there is no substitute for hands-on learning that takes place in the home and is customized to individual parents' and children's needs. Many intellectually disabled people find abstraction difficult, and may have trouble connecting classroom exercises real-world tasks. In-home services take instruction out of the abstract and into the here-and-now. Home visitors can also spot problems sooner than a case manager might—for example, a pile of unopened bills or an empty refrigerator. The disadvantage of home visiting is that service users may see these visits—justifiably—as an invasion of privacy. However, the intrusion can be minimized by scheduling visits around the parent's time constraints and being respectful of the parent's home.

Case Management

Material concerns can be overwhelming. Case managers are there to problem-solve and connect clients to resources in their communities. A good case manager can allow clients to focus their limited time and energy on the tasks of parenting rather than on deciphering the public benefits system or filling out forms. Even if you are not a case manager yourself, you may find it appropriate to provide limited case management services in your role as a teacher, therapist, or program staff member. Being knowledgeable about your area's social services resources and making referrals as needed will add to your potential to help your clients. It is not difficult to keep up to date about your community's resources. Joining online groups for social work and human services professionals can put you in reach of helpful organizations and people who are knowledgeable about what is available to your clients.

Domestic Violence Services

As outlined in Chapter 2, intellectually disabled people can be highly susceptible to abuse. The precise degree to which intellectually disabled people are more prone to experiencing domestic violence is unknown, but the lifetime rate of prevalence is estimated to be significantly higher than among the general population, at least among women (McCarthy et al., 2016). Abusers take advantage of people they perceive as vulnerable, and an intellectual disability is a common vulnerability to exploit. In Booth and Booth's (1997) qualitative survey of adults who grew up with intellectually disabled parents, of the 16 participants (out of 30 total) who reported having been abused as children, nine reported having experienced abuse at the hands of their fathers, and none reported abuse by their mothers. Only one abusive father was intellectually disabled; the rest were non-disabled. The other eleven abuse cases involved a stepfather or stepmother. These experiences speak to a great need for professionals to be vigilant about the possibility of domestic violence in such families. This also speaks to a structural need for domestic violence services, including shelters that can accommodate disabled people.

Acknowledgement of Strengths

It is easy to fall into the trap of thinking that intellectual disabilities are solely an impairment to parenting if you have little experience with disabled parents. However, intellectually disabled people can contribute much to parenting that those without disabilities may find more difficult, especially with children who are also intellectually disabled. In an article in *The Atlantic*, Sarah DeWeerdt (2017) profiles several autistic parents who bring skills to the parenting of both autistic and non-autistic children that parents who are not autistic may not even conceive of:

> 'As an autistic parent [of an autistic child], I'm in a unique situation of being able to have an insight into where they're coming from, what they're thinking and feeling,' says Johnson. When her oldest daughter was about 8, Johnson recalls, she used to get in trouble at school for putting her head down on the ground when the class sat on the floor. It turned out that the girl was 'listening' to the teacher in the next classroom through the vibrations.
>
> Johnson intuitively understood the situation. 'On one level, as a parent, you're like, "Well, you need to pay attention in class,"' Johnson says. 'On the other level, you have a real empathy for how that makes perfect sense, as crazy as it may sound.' Johnson remembers doing unusual things when she herself was a child, such as feeling compelled to perform an action the same number of times with her right and left hands.
>
> (DeWeerdt, 2017)

In the same article, another autistic parent, Drew, whose child is not autistic, talks about the conscious effort he puts into being a warm, thoughtful parent, even while struggling with the understandably overwhelming demands of raising a small child. Drew, whose own father parented with rigidity that Drew believes may have been the result of undiagnosed autism, used his knowledge of his condition to deliberately challenge his instincts:

> [Drew] says his own father probably had autism. He remembers longing for praise, but his father would instead critique the drawings he brought home from preschool: 'Move the eyes a bit over, and the nose is the wrong shape.'
>
> The possibility that his child might similarly suffer gave him pangs—and Drew determined to alter his behavior in certain ways. He forces himself to go to child-friendly events with bright colors and loud sounds even though he finds them overwhelming, for example. He suppresses the urge to cringe when his daughter's hands are covered with applesauce or oatmeal, not wanting her to pick up his abhorrence of mess and mushy textures. And he gushes over every piece of artwork his daughter produces. The irony is that his awareness of having a condition that makes it difficult for him to express affection has transformed virtually his every action into an expression of love.
>
> (DeWeerdt, 2017)

In your own practice, you may find that your clients put a great deal of effort into being conscientious parents—perhaps out of the well-justified fear that they will be unfairly perceived by others as incompetent, or perhaps because they have become experts at knowing and accommodating their own limitations. Many non-disabled parents think little about their own parenting practices and ways of making up for their skill deficits, but you will not meet many intellectually disabled parents with this attitude. In addition, an atmosphere of acceptance of disability and difference can also contribute to successful parenting. A household with a disabled parent will be much less likely to stigmatize disability, which can certainly not be said for every household.

Finite Length and Gradual Fading of Support

Throughout the training process, clients must be able to see a clear path toward increased autonomy. Your clients may complain to you of feeling overprogrammed. These feelings are understandable: after all, many intellectually disabled people attend day programs, job training, appointments with therapists, psychiatric visits, or other programming in addition to parenting training. This may lead them to feel vulnerable and constantly scrutinized, with no room to make mistakes in the way that other people do. For this reason, any parenting training must lead to greater responsibility. Clients must be able to say, "I will be done with parenting skills training (or done with the more intensive part of such training, or ready to move to the maintenance stage of such training, etc.) when I acquire X, Y, and Z skills." There must also be benchmarks on the way to completion, such as a reduction of service hours, movement to a higher-level or mainstream parenting class, or a gradual takeover of parenting responsibilities from a grandparent or other caregiver. Depending on the confines of the specific training program, and depending on whether it is mandated or voluntary, you may have more or less leeway on this, but it is crucial to at least discuss what your client's version of success might look like so that clients will not feel discouraged or stagnant.

Apply Your Skills With Case Study #4a: Beatrice and Will

Beatrice, age 22, is your new client at the Oak Street Clinic, where you work as an individual and family therapist. You learn from Beatrice's intake assessment that she experienced traumatic brain injury as a toddler, and that she is the mother of a one-year-old boy, Will. Beatrice lives with her parents, Greg and Deborah, who help her care for her Will. The child's father is not involved in his care and lives several states away. In subsequent conversations with Beatrice, you learn that your city's child protective services agency was briefly involved with the family three months after his birth when Beatrice, who was home alone with her son, allowed him to fall from a changing table. When Beatrice's parents returned home and learned what had happened, they took

Will to a local hospital, and though he was not seriously hurt, a hospital social worker alerted CPS after Beatrice described the incident truthfully. Though the case has since been closed, Greg and Deborah have grown more protective of Will and do not allow Beatrice to stay home alone with him. Beatrice is frustrated by this and confides to you that their lack of trust in her makes her sad and angry. Beatrice is proud of the childcare skills she has developed and enjoys caring for her son, but feels that she is not a "real" mother because she relies so much on her parents. Though she is developing new skills rapidly, she believes that her parents have not adjusted their level of trust in her accordingly.

1. You learn that there is a peer support group for intellec- tually disabled parents in your city. What could peer sup- port do for Beatrice? What is unique about peer support that other interventions might not provide?
2. You may have a hard time checking your assumptions about Beatrice's apparent lack of safety skills. What could explain the changing table incident other than Beatrice's disability? Might this have happened to a non-disabled parent?
3. If Beatrice's parents were to participate in a family ther- apy session with you, how would you help her voice be heard? You don't have to be a family therapist to answer this question. Identify some basic listening, facilitation, and advocacy skills you've used in your practice that may be helpful in centering Beatrice's experiences.
4. Think about some of the features of parenting programs for intellectually disabled people you learned about above, such as in-vivo services and gradual fading of support. Which ones stand out to you as potentially most beneficial to Beatrice if she were to enroll in such a program?

Apply Your Skills With Case Study #4b: Jackie and Wendy

You run a support group for LGBTQ parents and prospective parents in your town. There, you encounter Jackie and Wendy, two women who met through an online forum for autistic people in the arts. They have been romantically involved for three years. Jackie lives in alone in a studio apartment and is pursuing a master's degree, while Wendy lives with her parents and works part-time in a bookstore. They would like to move in with each other as soon as this is financially possible. Both are in agreement that they eventually want to become parents, but their attitudes toward parenting are as different as their personalities. Jackie often has trouble with noise and disruption of her routine, and worries that having a child will take away her quiet and orderly environment. She also has experienced being perceived as "cold" or "unemotional" by friends and coworkers, and is anxious about the possibility that her child will perceive her this way, too. Wendy, by contrast, believes that being an autistic parent will make her a stronger one. She feels a strong need to make her future child's life different from her own childhood, as she remembers fighting to be understood by her parents, who still do not fully comprehend her needs. Both partners are concerned about finances, but while Wendy is concerned about missing her window of opportunity to be a parent and wants to have children right after they move in together, Jackie thinks they should wait for more stability. Wendy thinks Jackie is being too negative about her autism diagnosis, while Jackie thinks Wendy is being unrealistic.

1. Where might Jackie go to find role models for successful parenting in autistic people? How might you encourage her to find these role models?
2. Financial burdens can weigh heavily on disabled parents, especially those who do not or cannot work full-time. What kinds of services would help lift these burdens? What is available in your own community? What kinds of preparation might Jackie and Wendy want to make before having a child?
3. Think about Drew, the autistic father we learned about earlier in this chapter. What skills did he bring to the table that non-autistic fathers may not? How did he mitigate behavior that he saw as interfering with parenting?

4. Wendy and Jackie are concerned about very different, but nonetheless valid things. How would you make sure that they both feel heard and validated? Remember that, although this chapter has encouraged optimism about disabled parenting, clients' own feelings about their parenting abilities and limitations should be treated with the utmost seriousness, even if they are negative feelings.

5

Sexual Orientation and Gender Identity

"I've got something to tell you about my life—my gay life."

This quote, taken from John D. Allen's *Gay, Lesbian, Bisexual, and Transgender People with Developmental Disabilities and Mental Retardation: Stories of the Rainbow Support Group*, comes from "Bill," a gay man whom the author met while facilitating a support group at the New Haven Pride Center designed for intellectually disabled LGBTQ people. Like many newly-out intellectually disabled people, Bill struggled with self-acceptance and found it difficult to socialize in the larger gay community. Despite these challenges, Bill was eager to share his newfound identity with others and to reach out to other gay people for companionship and support. The support group provided a much-needed source of validation and acceptance. "Homosexuality, that's okay, isn't it?" he asked in one session. "When we die, we go to heaven and that's where my soul will see that it's OK" (Allen, 2003).

This chapter will introduce you to the research available on LGBTQ identities in intellectually disabled people and provide a practical walk-through of client needs you may be asked to meet. As in previous chapters, our motto will be "proactive, not reactive." It won't be enough to raise these topics only when clients reveal themselves to be LGBTQ or ask questions about LGBTQ people in the media. They may not even get to that point if they think you'll react negatively. Instead, information and positive imagery about LGBTQ identities should be woven into the fabric of your work.

Why LGBTQ positivity?

When you start to bring LGBTQ positivity into your practice setting, you may meet with resistance. Other staff members might ask, "Why bring these topics up at all? What good will it do our clients to talk about sexual orientation and gender identity?" For fear of controversy, many programs may shun discussion of LGBTQ topics if clients do not bring them up. You yourself may wonder why engaging with sexuality and gender with your clients might benefit them in everyday life. The answers below will prepare you not just to rationalize your efforts to other staff members, but to focus your work on specific areas of client need.

Normalization

There is no question that your clients will receive conflicting messages about sexual orientation and gender expression. Family members, peers, staff members, television shows, books, and newspapers will bombard your clients with different signals about the acceptability of certain behaviors and identities. If your goal is for LGBTQ clients to feel comfortable and safe, your staff must do everything possible to make your program a place where LGBTQ identities are a familiar part of the landscape. If you're LGBTQ yourself, this might be a good time to reflect on the kind of support and encouragement you found helpful when you first began to explore your identity. If you aren't, you might want to think about the messages you received about LGBTQ people growing up and how this shaped your perceptions of what a man, woman, couple, or family should look like. What films and TV shows did you watch with queer people? Did you see LGBTQ businesses in your neighborhood? Did you hear about them at school or church? These reflections will help you become more aware of the tone you and your coworkers are setting.

Community

Even if your clients are perfectly comfortable in their identities, and even if they have supportive friends and loving families, they might have few or no friends who share the same identity. Without support, this means no opportunity to form romantic relationships, commune with people who have shared the same experience, or to experience the many facets of queer culture. The last thing may seem like a low priority if a client is struggling with things like poverty or illness, but don't discount the kinds of fulfillment that can come from finding art and music that speaks to you or finding out that people like you have existed throughout history. You may have to be the one to help your clients make these connections, whether to local LGBTQ organizations, gathering places, community events, pride marches, or online communities.

Safety

Clients will not seek help from staff members in danger situations if they feel that coming out to staff is itself dangerous. Those who are afraid of prejudiced staff members may not speak up if they fall victim to abuse or exploitation by romantic partners, for example. Fearing exposure and ridicule, they may keep these relationships secret from the professionals who are ostensibly there to protect and support them. If a client feels that they are not "supposed" to be having sex, they may seek it out in ways that are unsafe and expose them to sexually transmitted diseases, and might resist seeking healthcare if they have sexual health concerns. A 2012 study (McLelland et al.) found that intellectually disabled LGBT youth reported to researchers that they had sex in places that they were not comfortable and were unlikely to engage in safe sex behaviors due to limitations on their autonomy.

Legal Compliance

Your locality may have laws prohibiting discrimination based on sexual orientation and gender identity in healthcare, education, and other settings. In the city of New York, for example, municipal law provides a wide variety of protections based on sexuality and gender identity to students, employees, patients, and many other categories of people, and provides a reporting structure for people to file complaints if their rights are violated. Needless to say, your program should welcome LGBTQ clients regardless of the legal implications, but the added pressure of these laws may prove useful when the time comes to justify your efforts to program management. Look up your local antidiscrimination laws and keep them on hand for reference.

General Knowledge

Perhaps your LGBTQ clients will benefit from LGBTQ-inclusive programming, but what about your other clients? Knowledge about the basics of sexuality and gender identity should be a part of everyone's repertoire. When your clients inevitably meet LGBTQ people, their response should not be confusion or disbelief. Familiarity with the existence of LGBTQ people should be considered as essential as that with the parts of the human body or the five senses.

Sexual Identity and Expression Needs

Whether they can articulate it or not, your clients will most likely feel some need for **participation** in the larger LGBTQ community. Your recently-out gay client may have learned of gay bars or dating apps. Your trans client may wonder what other trans people look like and how they live their lives. This goes hand in hand with the need for **romantic companionship**, which LGBTQ clients—unlike your other clients—may not be able to find without deliberately seeking out groups of people with similar identities. Ideally, your program's usual outings to shopping malls and bowling alleys could be supplemented with trips to LGBTQ community centers or gay businesses such as bars, bookstores, and cafes. However, this could be complicated by the fact that many residential or day program settings have limited staff, who may not be able to organize an outing unless there is universal interest. Staff may be uncomfortable, or even prohibited from, leading outings to gay bars and nightclubs, even though these places represent a major source of culture and community for many LGBTQ people. For clients who travel independently, residences might restrict the times that residents can leave or return, preventing them from socializing in the evening in ways that typical adults take for granted. In Bennett & Coyle's (2007) "A minority within a minority: Experiences of gay men with intellectual disabilities," published in *Out in Psychology*, the authors interviewed gay-identified intellectually disabled men living in residential settings and learned about the challenges they face in going to gay venues:

> 'I just went dancing . . . and the day after I went back to the [residence]. They told me off and said, "You're not allowed to go out for the day."'
> 'The only problem in here is that staff like me back before it gets too late. They go to bed about eleven. Some staff go [to bed] about ten they do.'
> 'I'll tell you, the whole of the staff at the Cedars [client's residence] knows everything. . . . All the other people, the residents know everything about where I go, who I go out with, this and that. . . . It's none of their business at all—it's private.'

Other participants described discomfort with bringing romantic partners to their residences, limited privacy, absence of friends to accompany them to gay venues, fear of violence and prejudice, difficulties navigating public transportation, and lack of knowledge about where to find gay venues. One interviewee even asked one of the interviewers to find out where the local gay bars could be found and report back to him! Strikingly, most of these concerns could be solved by staff who talk openly about LGBTQ issues and care about clients' need for community and companionship, supported by program management that is responsive and flexible. Few programs can boast this, but even if you are the only staff member willing to advocate for LGBTQ residents, your clients will benefit greatly.

Clients who are sexually active, or anticipate becoming sexually active, will have **safer sex** needs. This is another area in which being proactive—making education and materials about safer sex (e.g. literature, condoms) available to all clients, regardless of your assumptions about their sexual orientation or particular type of sexual activity—makes much more sense than providing these things after you've learned that someone has had an unsafe sexual encounter. The physical environment of your practice setting can make it easier or more difficult to provide these materials. Clients may understandably feel hesitant about taking materials that might be embarrassing, disease-related, or related to an identity or activity that they may not be ready to share with the world (e.g. dental dams for a lesbian-identified client). These materials can be placed in private or secluded areas, such as a bathroom or a quiet corridor, to encourage uptake.

Many of the needs mentioned above could be met with **group support**. An LGBTQ support group, whether specific to intellectually disabled clients or based in the community, provides the most important benefit of all: exposure to others in the LGBTQ community, which means access to information, resources, affirmation, and companionship. You may choose to start one yourself if there is enough interest among clients of your organization (or if you feel ambitious enough to take it on as a personal project in the community), or you may refer your client to an existing group—see the resource listings in Appendix C for more information on how to find these.

Toolbox: LGBTQ Support Group

You have a meeting space and a stack of spiffy flyers—let's start a group! These steps will help you get started.

- Decide on the purpose of your group. What kinds of support and resources will your group provide? Examples might include:
  - Information (e.g. about local LGBTQ events, relevant news, bars and clubs)

- ◆ Discussion and support (e.g. coming out, exploring one's sexuality, navigating LGBTQ communities as a disabled person)
- ◆ Creative expression (e.g. art classes, poetry readings, karaoke nights, group newsletter)
- ◆ Celebrations and fun (e.g. parties, movie nights, dances)
- ◆ Trips and excursions (e.g. to LGBTQ museums, bookstores, bars, meetups, political demonstrations)
- ◆ Education (e.g. healthy relationships, safe sex, knowing one's rights)
- ◆ Public self-expression (e.g. flags, pins, stickers)

- ◆ Decide how to structure your group. It could be as simple as an hour-long, open-ended discussion about participants' lives and struggles. However, even if you decide on a more informal structure, it may prove useful to divide the group time into sections, each with a pre-defined task—for example, a five-minute intro session for new members, or ten minutes of information about local LGBTQ events. This may be especially beneficial to clients who have difficulty with transitioning from one activity to another, as it provides a consistent, familiar format from week to week.

- ◆ Set up ground rules about expected behavior and explain them in clear language at the start of each session. For greater buy-in, ask participants at the start of the group what they'd like the group rules to be. Gain consensus and write up a rule poster with the group's collaboration. Leave room for more rules and continue to ask for feedback as the group develops further and gains new members.

- ◆ Use group check-ins to gauge whether participants feel safe, happy, and comfortable in your group, or to see how they've been feeling in general. A check-in about the group should feel informal and low-stakes (for example, "Let's go around the circle and each talk about how you feel about being in this group," or simply, "How is your week so far?").

You might even choose to use a simple scale to measure how participants are doing, such as, "On a scale of one to ten, how do safe do you feel in this group?" or "Pick a face sticker that shows how you're feeling right now."

◆ Add incentives for showing up. Coffee and donuts will increase your attendance in a way that few things will. As an added bonus, participants who are shy about outing themselves to other clients as LGBTQ, or who are simply curious about the LGBTQ community, can maintain a plausible excuse for being there—perhaps they only wanted a free snack!

◆ Be prepared to follow up with program administration about what you hear in the group. If you learn that group participants experience bullying from other clients or have problems with parental acceptance, share this information with your colleagues and respond on an individual or program-wide level.

◆ Pay close attention to the demographic makeup of your group. In Allen's (2003) book about his experiences with the Rainbow Support Group, he writes about one early problem the group faced: women would attend one session of the group and never return. Your group may face a similar situation. Perhaps you'll find that trans people, for example, or people of color feel uncomfortable attending for more than one session. This may have to do with a lack of others like them in the group, a particularly strident or offensive group member, or topics that aren't relevant to their interests. If possible, speak to the group member about their reasons for leaving so that you can incorporate their feedback into future sessions (and hopefully welcome them back).

Gender Identity Needs

Intellectually disabled trans people face a complex set of challenges in navigating both the LGBTQ community and the world at large. Seeking to understand more about these challenges, I turned to Cerridwyn Donaldson, a trans woman with Prader-Willi syndrome who volunteered to be interviewed via instant messaging about her experiences.[1] Cerridwyn lives in a residence operated by a non-profit agency and is a fierce self-advocate: "For the most part, I do feel my needs [related to transitioning] have been met. Mainly, because I basically won't take no for an answer" (Personal communication, October 1, 2017). However, she often feels that staff members do not take her wishes about when and how to come out into account:

> I am not given the opportunity to come out to my staff. [My residence] informs every potential staff person that I am trans. So all staff I work with already know by the time they start receiving training. . . . There is something I wish they would do better, and that is leaving it to me to come out. Although, it doesn't bring any safety concerns. As my SLS [Supportive Living Services] agency wouldn't hire anyone who is transphobic to work with me. But it doesn't allow my staff to get to know me as a person/client. Rather than a person/client that is trans. This hurts because being transgender doesn't define me, it's just a part of who I am. Thus, my SLS agency telling my staff makes it seem as if being trans does define me.
>
> (Personal communication, October 1, 2017)

Cerridwyn also feels that her parents sometimes do not respect her wishes around privacy and other matters, even though they are generally supportive of her transition:

> [M]y parents [allow] my pre-transition photos be present. They hang on the walls at their house. I truly feel close to breaking down all the way to sobbing every time I see them. For it reminds me of the intense pain, I went through not being able to be me. Also it basically outs me to anyone who is over at my parents' house whether they

know or not. I don't want myself or others to see them
EVER. I have talked to my parents about keeping them
to the privacy of in their room. As well as being packed
away in a box, that they can look at, if they need to. My
parents told me they were more than happy to do so but
it has not been done. I sometimes wonder if it's because
of my disability. I feel they might think my request is less
valid or less important. For I don't feel as strong about it
as I could. Like, I only asked because many of my trans
friends have requested the same of their parents. So I am
going along with the flow.

(Personal communication, October 1, 2017)

Though Cerridwyn feels that she is the same person that
she was before transition, and that she has always been female
no matter what her body looked like, her friends and family
do not always respect her feelings about this. She has requested that they not refer to her as male when talking about her
pre-transition self, but they continue to talk about her past in
ways that upset her. She attributes this at least partially to her
disability:

The majority of my friends and family think that I was
this other person. Thus, now I am a different person. The
person I was meant to be. I have told people numerous
times my feelings. But it seems nothing changes. I feel
once again this goes back to my disability. This time,
as a result of myself being so open about my disability.
That I would be so open about my pre-transition self. But
I need people to know I have always been one person,
who is female, and is named Cerridwyn. It upsets me
that people think my disability changes how people feel
about my needs.

(Personal communication, October 1, 2017)

Self-determination and autonomy are also needs that often
go unmet for Cerridwyn. Her parents are legally involved in
many aspects of her life, and because of this involvement, they

participate in her transition in ways that are often unwanted or unnecessary:

> I do not feel like my privacy and autonomy [needs have] been met at all. [M]y disability [requires] me to be legally conserved. My parents have had the legal right to know, be involved in, and have a say in, every part of my transition. I have had moments where my parents spoke with my doctors without asking me first if I am okay with it. [E]ven if a disabled person has a conservatorship, they have full rights to privacy and autonomy. Just as anyone without one would. I don't feel like conservatorships should extend as far as a disabled trans person's transition. I feel this is something the individual transitioning should have full control over.
>
> (Personal communication, October 1, 2017)

As Cerridwyn's experiences demonstrate, trans-identified intellectually disabled people have the same needs as trans people in the general population, but often struggle to get these needs met, due in no small part to the dual marginalization they face. Sometimes this occurs because their concerns are not taken seriously; at other times, financial and logistical challenges get in the way. In Cerridwyn's case, the accommodation and understanding that she requests would cost nothing and provide immense benefit, but her staff and family members still struggle to meet her needs. If this is the case with your clients, count yourself lucky—you can provide them with a safe and welcoming environment solely with interventions like advocacy and staff training without calling on your organization for scarce resources. This section is devoted to the needs of intellectually disabled people with respect to their gender identity, and how you can help meet them whatever your role.

Many of the needs of transgender clients center on the need for **recognition** of their identified gender. This simply means that a client who identifies as male, for example, should be addressed by his chosen name and pronouns, given access to clothing that fits his identity, and allowed to participate in activities and groups for male clients (if your agency *must* segregate these by gender). This also means speaking up every time staff or other clients misgender or "deadname" (use an old name for) your client or fail to acknowledge their gender identity. Recognition alone may count for a large part of your intervention—you may be surprised at the level of ignorance and resistance to recognizing clients' identities you find among even well-trained staff members.

Transgender clients will be in need of specialized **medical care**, even if they do not plan to medically transition. Transgender healthcare includes not only care related to transition, but engaging with trans-friendly providers for everyday healthcare needs. If a client does wish to receive hormones and gender-affirming surgeries, obtaining these services may be complex, especially in rural or more conservative areas. In the past, it was often difficult or impossible for intellectually disabled people to medically transition due to the belief that they could not provide medical consent or lack a full understanding of their own gender identity. Today, gender clinics increasingly provide intellectually disabled clients with a full spectrum of services, though it is typical to require more evaluation than for non-disabled clients. Medicare and some state Medicaid programs must now cover transgender services, including surgery, though the 2016 presidential election has thrown these coverage rules into jeopardy as of this writing. It may be wise to keep up on these developments for the sake of disseminating information to your clients.

Some level of trans-affirmative **mental healthcare** will likely be needed. If your client plans to medically transition, doctors who provide hormone therapy or surgery typically require a letter from a mental health professional. The World Professional Association for Transgender Health (WPATH) publishes a set of widely-accepted guidelines for therapists who treat trans clients, especially concerning the provision of such letters. The organization's proposed requirements for receiving hormone therapy and surgery have loosened in recent years, and many therapists do not follow the WPATH criteria, feeling that the organization's recommendations are outdated and place too high a burden on trans clients to "prove" their authenticity. Even if trans clients do not plan to seek transition-related medical care, therapy might be useful to help the client cope with the process of coming out and seeking recognition, and to discuss and clarify aspects of their identity if desired.

Gender expression needs include prosthetics (e.g. breast forms), trans-specific items of clothing (e.g. binders), makeup, nail polish, clothing, and accessories (e.g. handbags, neckties, hair clips). As you may have guessed, these needs are often material and cannot always be funded with health insurance. Talk to local trans organizations or find information on the internet about where clients can procure needed items. Clothing banks and thrift stores may be able to help with apparel and accessories— see Appendix C for national resources on this topic.

As with other LGBTQ clients, a trans client may need help **coming out**. Clients may ask you to help them tell others about their new name and pronouns and deal with others' reactions. This means that you may need to do some level of client and staff education beforehand, especially if your client may have trouble navigating negative reactions or intrusive questions. A common concern may be whether the client is "really" trans or has thought through the implications of transitioning. Remember that the fact that your client has come out to you means that they have likely done a great deal of soul-searching and introspection. You do not have to convince anyone of the authenticity of your client's experience—only that your client's gender identity is their own business and that questioning its reality is unhelpful and demeaning. Caution must be used to protect your client's **privacy** if they are not yet openly trans, or not out to everyone in every setting. Even if your client *is* open about their gender identity, the details of their identity should not be discussed in front of others without their permission. If you would not discuss such details about a coworker or a friend, do not do so with your clients' details.

Legal assistance may also be needed if your client elects to change their name or gender marker. Unfortunately, the process of doing so is different for every state and involves multiple agencies, including the state's department of motor vehicles (for photo ID), the state's department of vital records (for birth certificate), the Social Security Administration (for social security records) and various other places such as the client's bank, doctor's office, or school. The process tends to require a high level of literacy and organization, which means that your clients may need your help or the help of a case manager. Some organizations can provide help with the process for free—see Appendix C for these resources.

Toolbox: Trans Vocabulary

If you have no experience working with trans-identified clients, you may stumble over common gender identity terms or fear offending someone, even if you yourself are a member of the LGBTQ community. You will need a full spectrum of terminology to talk about gender identity with your clients, and may even need to teach them words to express the complexity of their experiences. Let's look at some common terms that you might encounter while working with trans clients.

◆ **AFAB/AMAB.** "Assigned female/male at birth." Used to denote the sex marker on one's birth certificate and/or the gender role in which one was raised as a child.
◆ **Binding.** Compressing one's chest to de-emphasize breasts and create a masculine silhouette. A **binder** is a garment that creates this effect. Binders commonly look like sports bras or athletic compression shirts.
◆ **Cisgender/cis.** Used to refer to people whose gender assigned at birth is the same as their identified gender (i.e. people who are not **transgender**).
◆ **Cross-dresser.** A person, usually male, who wears clothing not traditionally associated with their gender for self-expression and/or sexual reasons. Cross-dressers typically do not wish to live full-time as the opposite gender. The term "transvestism/transvestite" is no longer considered appropriate. Trans people wearing clothing of their identified gender are not considered to be

cross-dressing; likewise, people who simply prefer to dress in a non-stereotypical way (e.g. butch lesbians) should not be referred to as cross-dressers unless they themselves use that term.

◆ **Drag queen.** A person, typically male, who wears traditionally female clothing as part of a performance. Trans women and cross-dressers should not be referred to as drag queens, though a few trans women do perform as drag queens.

◆ **Dysphoria.** Feelings of discomfort with one's body, appearance, or role.

◆ **Gender-confirming surgery.** Surgery related to one's gender identity, which may include procedures on one's breasts/chest, genitals, face, or voice. Terms like "sex reassignment surgery" and "sex change" are no longer used. Not all transgender people desire surgery, and surgery is not necessary to be an "authentic" member of one's identified gender.

◆ **Genderfluid.** Used to describe gender identity that is not fixed and can change depending on time, mood, or other factors.

◆ **Genderqueer, gender neutral, agender, bigender, non-binary, third gender, androgyne.** These words are all used to describe people whose gender identity cannot be wholly encompassed in the terms "male" or "female." These terms have evolved over the years and can mean different things to different people.

◆ **Hormone replacement therapy.** The administration of hormones (e.g. testosterone, estrogen, anti-androgens) to produce the secondary sex characteristics of one's identified gender. Not all transgender people undergo hormone therapy.

◆ **Misgendering.** Referring to someone by the wrong pronouns or name. If in doubt, ask your clients what they prefer.

◆ **Packing.** Wearing a prosthetic penis ("packer") under one's clothing.

- **Passing.** Being seen as a member of one's identified gender. Can also be used to mean being seen as a cisgender person. Some trans people dislike this term, as it can imply deception. Today, the trans community places less emphasis on the importance of "passing" in public and more on becoming comfortable with one's body and appearance. A more precise term is "**visibly/not visibly trans**."
- **Stealth.** The state of hiding one's transgender status, often out of fear of discrimination. Can apply to certain contexts; for example, a trans person might be stealth at work, but out among friends. Do not use this term to refer to a trans person's visibility unless they themselves use it.
- **Top surgery/bottom surgery.** Refers to gender-confirming surgery on the chest area and the genital area respectively.
- **Trans, transgender.** These words are used to describe someone who identifies as a gender other than the one assigned at birth. These words can also be broadly used to encompass anyone whose gender identity or expression does not precisely match their gender assigned at birth. The word "transsexual" was once widely used, but has fallen out of favor, and "transgender" or "trans" are the current preferred terms. The terms **MTF/FTM** (male-to-female/female-to-male) are still used, but are less common, as they place undue emphasis on one's outward change rather than one's inner identity.
- **Trans man, trans woman.** "Trans man" is used to describe someone who was assigned female at birth and identifies as male, while "trans woman" is used to describe someone who was assigned male and identifies as female. These terms should be used as separate words and not compounded as "transwoman/transman," as these terms can be taken to imply that trans women and men are not "real" women/men. Some people use the term "man/woman with a trans history."

◆ **Transition.** The process of changing one's body, outward presentation, and legal status. Not all trans people use this term to describe their experiences.

Questions for Self-Reflection

These questions are primarily intended for those who do not identify as LGBTQ. However, they may be illuminating for those who do, especially in reflecting on your coming out process and the ways in which you first encountered LGBTQ life, both positive and negative.

1. Where did you first learn about the existence of LGBTQ people (e.g. schoolmates, television, magazines, conversations with adults)? Were the messages positive or negative? Did you believe them? Did these messages affect how you saw LGBTQ people you met after that? Did you intentionally or unintentionally say anything hurtful as a result?
2. Who was the first trans person you encountered? If you don't personally know any trans people, think about trans people you may have seen in the media, such as Lana Wachowski (co-director of the *Matrix* films) or Laverne Cox (Sophia in *Orange is the New Black*). What was your initial reaction to hearing their stories? Be honest with yourself, even if your reaction was negative.
3. Think back to questions your clients have asked you or other staff members about sexuality and gender identity. What questions made you uncomfortable and why? What questions were you unable to answer, either due to lack of information or embarrassment? How do you think your reaction affected your clients?
4. What messages, implicit or explicit, have you received from your supervisor about LGBTQ identities in your practice? Your coworkers? Clients' parents and families? How have these messages affected staff attitudes around sexual orientation and gender identity in your practice?

5. Think about the use of humor in your practice setting. Are jokes, even ones that sound harmless to you, ever made about clients' sexuality? Their gender presentation? How do you react when these jokes are made? What do you think your clients would say if they heard them?

Apply Your Skills With Case Study #5: Tracy

You are a direct support staff member at Ocean House, a group residence for intellectually disabled people in a large city. You have been on staff for three years and have established trusting relationships with all twelve of its residents, including Tracy, a 35-year-old who moved to the group residence from her parents' home two months ago. You are surprised when Tracy takes you aside one day and confides to you that she is "like Maura, but the other way around" referring to a transgender woman from the TV show *Transparent*, which some residents have been watching lately. Haltingly, Tracy requests to be referred to by male pronouns. Tracy also expresses the desire to wear male clothing. You agree to call Tracy by his preferred pronouns. However, the conversation ends on an awkward note; you ask no follow-up questions and do not mention the conversation to anyone else on staff. You feel overwhelmed and out of your depth, as you have not worked with trans clients in any capacity. (If you are more experienced with trans issues, imagine that you are supervising or advising this staff member). In fact, you are not even sure if "transgender" is how Tracy would describe himself. You wonder whether Tracy has come out to other residents or staff. You wonder whether it is okay to bring this to the attention of your supervisor, to call Tracy by his preferred pronouns in front of others, or to ask Tracy the many questions that are flooding your mind right now. You wonder whether Tracy will decide to change his name or to medically transition.

1. How can you protect Tracy's confidentiality? Is it okay to bring the subject up with your supervisor? Your coworkers? Tracy's parents? Other residents? (Remember that it

is Tracy who bears the consequences of any confidentiality decisions you make. Also consider the possible legal implications of violating Tracy's privacy).

2. You decide to talk to Tracy further about the things he told you about his gender identity. What questions might you ask? Remember that the questions you ask should be directly relevant to your care of Tracy, and that questions meant merely to satisfy your curiosity might be confusing or unhelpful. What do you need to know about Tracy to treat him with respect and compassion? What might Tracy's gender identity needs be and how can you find out what they are? Ask open-ended questions and don't assume that Tracy has a particular need without confirming this with him.

3. What resources in your community could be helpful to Tracy? If you don't know of any, look on the internet for local LGBTQ resource guides or ask other professionals in your field. You can find LGBTQ resources and many others in Appendix C.

4. What can you do to make the group home more welcoming to people like Tracy? Remember that not all LGBTQ clients will have the same needs or specific identity as Tracy does. Think of ways you can accomplish this on an individual level (changing your own practice) and on an organizational level (changing your organization's policies and practices, changing the physical environment of your practice setting, changing the way staff are trained).

Note

1 Prader-Willi syndrome is a genetic disorder characterized by constant hunger that is usually associated with social difficulties to some degree, though not always impairment in general intelligence.

6

Sexual Offending

"I don't really feel the need to defend my job," asserts an anonymous Australian support worker for intellectually disabled men who have sexually offended in a 2015 *Vice* article. "[I want] to educate people on the realities of this group of people." The author goes on to note that many people don't see the need for this type of work, or have misconceptions about the risk posed by these men: "When I tell people about my work they're usually surprised and concerned for me. They have the idea that I'm in danger, as if these guys are mad offending machines." The author relates the difficulties of working with this population, even in a country with a robust mental healthcare and social services infrastructure compared to the United States:

> The work is obviously very challenging, but not how you might expect. It's hard to create normality in an environment that's artificial. We're trying to show them how to develop relationships and daily rituals but they're under 24-hour care and supervision. They need to sign out when they leave and call us when they're in the community. If they drive, we check the mileage on their cars.

> They've got to be home by a certain time; we lock their windows and alarm their doors. There's a strange power dynamic—I'm a 28-year-old girl telling a 45-year-old man he can't do what he wants.
>
> (Anonymous, as told to Wendy Syfret, 2015)

The author also highlights some of the factors that go into sexual offending in intellectually disabled people, noting that a history of trauma is very common in this population. She also notes the population's alarmingly high rate of sexual abuse:

> Most of the guys I work with have come from incredibly traumatic places themselves. People with a disability or a mental illness are very vulnerable to abuse. Of the people I work with, probably 95 out of 100 were abused by family or while in state care. As children they learnt those are normal behaviours and that's the way adults express love.
>
> (Anonymous, as told to Wendy Syfret, 2015)

For intellectually disabled people who engage in sexual offending behaviors, the world can be an unforgiving place. Little is understood about sexual offending as it relates to intellectually disabled people: their reasons for offending, the rates at which they offend, the risk factors that lead to their offending, or their victim profiles. Furthermore, misconceptions about the sexual dangerousness of intellectually disabled people create a high level of stigma; those who realize that their behavior is problematic, or whose problem behavior is detected by their families, may not get the care they need due to this stigma. They may see no alternative path to healthy sexuality or have few role models to guide them.

In the following sections, you will learn about the (admittedly scant) research that exists on sexual offending in intellectually disabled people, and the treatment options that may be available to them. If you are interested in learning more about the treatment resources available to your clients, Appendix C lists the contact information for agencies that deal with these issues and may be able to provide you with referrals.

Research and Statistics on Sexual Offending

Useful statistics on the rate of sexual offending in intellectually disabled people are hard to come by. Although rates of sexual offending behavior have been measured to be slightly higher in the intellectually disabled population than in the general population in some studies, other studies show no such correlation (Craig & Hutchinson, 2005; Lindsay, 2002). It is difficult to compare rates of sexual offending among intellectually disabled people to those of intellectually typical people, as researchers can only measure offenses that have been detected by others or self-reported, and thus the rates may be affected by reporting bias. It is possible that it is more difficult for intellectually disabled people to conceal their sexual offenses than the general population, for example, or that the particular offenses more common among intellectually disabled people are less detectable. Lindsay (2002) also suggests that sexual abuse in childhood may conduce to greater rates of sexual offending; as we saw in Chapter 2, intellectually disabled people are highly vulnerable to sexual abuse at all ages.

Among those who offend, types of offense vary, and most victims are known to the perpetrator. McBrien (2003) found that in a sample of 1,326 intellectually disabled adults known to a local health authority in the United Kingdom, 26% had engaged in risky sexual behaviors that may have been sexual offenses; researchers defined these behaviors as soliciting for sexual activity, sexually approaching adults, sexually approaching children, or undressing or exposing oneself in public. In a study of 103 intellectually disabled sexual offenders in the state of Vermont, McGrath (2007) found that 27.2% had committed sexual assault, 17.5% had molested female child victims, 27.2% had molested male child victims, 11.7% had engaged in incest, and 16.5% were non-contact offenders (e.g. those who had engaged in behavior that did not involve physical contact, such as public masturbation and exposure). Child and adult strangers represented only 10.7% and 9.7% of victims, respectively. Unfortunately, there appears to be little current research on intellectually disabled sexual offenders who are not male. The McGrath (2007) study referenced above indicated that the seven female offenders served by the Vermont state offenders' program were excluded from the study. This seems to reflect a much lower likelihood of offense, but may also potentially reflect a lower likelihood of detection due to stereotypes about women as perpetrators of sexual offenses.

If there *is* a genuine disparity between the rates of sexual offending in the intellectually disabled and general population, its cause is unclear. Various researchers have contended that a lack of sexual knowledge may drive inappropriate sexual behavior among intellectually disabled men—known in the research literature as "counterfeit deviance" and thought to be easily remediable by sex education and counseling. In this view, a certain percentage of intellectually disabled offenders are thought not to possess the same qualities as do intellectually typical offenders who commit the same offenses. However, Michie (2006) casts doubt on this hypothesis, finding that intellectually disabled people who sexually offended have a *higher* level of sexual knowledge than non-offenders as measured by the Socio-Sexual Knowledge and Attitudes Tool–Revised (SSKAAT–R). In a similar study, Lockhart et al. (2010) found that intellectually disabled adults of both genders who displayed challenging behaviors of a sexual nature had higher sexual knowledge than, and the same level of sexual experience (also measured by the SSKAAT–R) as, a control group of intellectually disabled adults without such behaviors. However, this does not mean that the subject of counterfeit deviance is settled. Griffiths et al. (2013) point out that people with histories of sexual offense may have been exposed to more sex education *as a result* of their offending behaviors, or may have been more interested in sex to begin with. In addition, there are factors other than lack of sexual knowledge that may contribute to offending behaviors in intellectually disabled people, such as lack of social skills and unmet sexual needs (Griffiths et al., 2013).

As a practical matter, though, the body of research on the subject of counterfeit deviance suggests that simple sex education is not enough to target sexually problematic behavior in intellectually disabled people. The same beliefs and motivations that cause the general population to offend likely contribute to offenses by intellectually disabled people to various degrees.

Likewise, improving social skills and increasing clients' opportunities to engage in healthy relationships may improve, but fail to fully address, these behaviors. It is always difficult to pinpoint one particular cause of offending behavior, and some behaviors can have many contributing factors, which means that therapy is appropriate in nearly all cases, if only to explore the client's motives more fully. As with intellectually typical offenders, therapy specific to problematic sexual behavior should be offered rather than general therapy.

Treatment for Intellectually Disabled Sexual Offenders

Like sex education, programs of treatment for sexual offending behaviors can be adapted to the specific needs of intellectually disabled people. Rose et al. (2002) found that group treatment for intellectually disabled men targeting attitudes related to sexual offending was effective at changing these attitudes and at increasing sexual knowledge, though attitudes tended to revert to previous levels after the intervention. Group members were not recorded to have offended one year after the intervention. Similarly, a later study (SOTSEC-ID, 2010) found that a year-long cognitive behavior therapy resulted in increased victim empathy and sexual knowledge and decreased cognitive distortions. These changes were found to be significant six months after treatment ended, and of the 48 men who initially enrolled in treatment, only four had reoffended one year after the end of treatment. Interestingly, 92% of participants stayed in treatment for the full year, even though only 57% of participants were required to attend by law, suggesting that participants were motivated to attend treatment by factors other than fear of legal consequences. Both studies were conducted solely with male participants. There appear to be no programs specifically for non-males who offend, and research in this area, as stated above, is practically nonexistent.

Unfortunately, it may be impossible for you to find a program in your local community that is tailored to this population.

Few programs for sex offenders are specific to intellectually disabled people. However, individual practitioners who treat sex offenders may have experience treating intellectually disabled people. Programs and clinics who specialize in treating offenders may also be able to adapt their programming to suit your clients' needs. Such programs do not typically require a great amount of literacy, and are usually based on some combination of individual and group therapy, which most people with basic verbal skills can manage. One of my former clients who participated in such a program was shy and had limited social skills, but was able to participate in groups with encouragement, and was open to engaging individually with clinicians, who reported that they felt that he was meaningfully participating in the program.

Pathology or Preference? Risk Factors That Aren't

It is important to note that not all sexual offending behaviors involve behaviors considered "deviant" or "fetishistic" by the general public, and there is no apparent correlation between these behaviors and sexual offending. It is therefore crucial not to stigmatize clients who engage in these behaviors as potential sexual offenders. As we saw in Chapter 3, the definition of "deviant" has changed greatly over time. Many sexual behaviors that are common and accepted today, such as BDSM or anal sex, would have been met with revulsion and derision 50 or 100 years ago, even by many mental health professionals. The vast majority of unusual sexual behaviors are harmless to others—and, indeed, can bring joy and fulfillment to the people who engage in them.

Other professionals with less knowledge about human sexuality (or perhaps more fear of it) may see your clients who engage in unusual sexual behavior as sexual threats to other clients or staff. They may try to prevent such behavior even if it occurs in private, or monitor those who engage in these behaviors more carefully than other clients, fearing that these clients will act out sexually toward others solely because of their non-mainstream interests. This will prove an excellent opportunity to advocate for your clients and to educate them about their sexual rights. As for your colleagues, it will be worthwhile to impress upon them that the way to prevent clients from being victimized is to have robust policies and training around the detection and prevention of sexual abuse (see Chapter 2), not by policing behavior that harms no one, and possibly destroying your clients' trust in them in the process.

In addition, simply talking about sex, even if it is inappropriate for the context, should not be considered a risk factor for sexual offending. Some clients may make sexual jokes and say words that they know will get a reaction from staff. (One of my former clients memorably loved to shout the word "underwear" at inopportune moments to get a laugh from staff members). Others may be curious about sexuality and use jokes to communicate real anxieties about sexuality, or to test whether they are "allowed" to talk about these topics. Still others may simply want to talk about sexuality openly as typical adults do with their friends. However, absent evidence of harassment or assaultive behaviors, there is nothing particularly concerning about sexual talk from a risk management standpoint. This is not to say that sexually inappropriate language or slurs should be ignored, especially if they target another client, but the appropriate response is to educate, counsel, set boundaries, and provide a safe forum for frank sexual discussion—not to immediately label the client as a potential sex offender.

Apply Your Skills With Case Study #6: Gray

You are a master's-level social worker at a large legal services organization. Your responsibility is to refer criminal justice clients to such services as mental health and drug treatment, social services, shelters, and benefits assistance. You have just been assigned a client, 20-year-old Gray, who was arrested earlier this week for touching women inappropriately on the bus and released on $5,000 bail yesterday. This is the second time he has been arrested for such behavior. You interview Gray and learn that he was born with Williams syndrome, received special education services throughout his time in school, loves his part-time job delivering food for a sandwich shop, and lives at home with his mother. You attempt to ask Gray questions about what happened on the bus, and though he is talkative about other subjects, he refuses to talk about the incident except to say that he feels that he "can't help it." Gray's attorney, Clark, would like to show the court that he is taking steps to address his behavior in the hope of receiving a reduced or alternative sentence. However, Clark is a recent law graduate and has little knowledge of what kind of sex offender treatment is available. Adding to your workload, Gray's mother and extended family members are constantly calling you and asking for information about how his case is going. These family members seem to be heavily involved in Gray's life and are convinced that he has been framed for the alleged sexual touching, though this is not his first arrest and the encounter on the bus was caught on tape from two different angles.

1. How would you go about learning if there is appropriate sex offender treatment in your area? If you found a program that looked suitable, what questions would you ask staff to determine whether it was the right fit for Gray? What kinds of skills (e.g. literacy, social skills) might Gray need to participate in the program? What strengths might Gray bring to treatment?

2. Considering Gray's family's involvement in his life, how can you protect his confidentiality? What might you say to family members who call about his case? Remember that the client is over the age of 18 and that his family members likely have no legal right to information. Remember also that the client's attorney may have specific legal reasons for you to keep quiet about the case.

3. Gray's family may be in denial about the seriousness of the accusations. What kinds of services could help them deal with what they have learned about Gray?

7

Disrupting the Language of Sexuality and Intellectual Disability

Previous chapters have focused primarily on specific areas of sexuality work, such as parenting and relationships. This chapter will discuss the overarching idea of how we talk about sexuality and intellectual disabilities and how such language (often inadvertently) shapes our practice. We may not immediately recognize the implications of our own words because we are immersed in them. The clinical jargon of your profession may have become second nature, and the particular phrases that your organization uses to describe clients and their lives may not carry any special meaning to you. However, these words and phrases may have unintentional effects on how you view your clients and your role. The weight of your language will be felt by your clients: whether you see them as decision-makers or subjects, experts or learners, independent or interdependent. The following is an exploration of several facets of the language of disability and sexuality. It is by no means comprehensive, but it will start you on the road to thinking more carefully about where your beliefs about these topics come from.

The Fallacy of Independence

The word "independence" is often used by well-meaning clinicians to talk about goal-setting with their clients. In practice, this usually sets the stage for a service regimen that is defined by a drive toward self-sufficiency, sometimes at the expense of other worthy goals. Addressing the concept of *inter*dependence, activist and writer Kathy Snow (2016) writes that the endless focus on independence in disability services places a disproportionate focus on achieving the "highest" level of independent functioning, regardless of the disabled person's own goals and preferences:

> [I]n the disability arena, many worship at the altar of "independence." A variety of disability organizations, special educators, families, and others have the goal of "helping people with disabilities achieve their highest level of independence." What does this statement mean? Independence in what form? Financial, physical, decision-making, or what? What if children or adults with disabilities have a different definition than those who promote this goal? What does "highest level" mean, and who defines it? How could the goal be achieved if there's no consensus on what the words mean?
>
> (Snow, 2016)

Indeed, the focus on independence may be one of the reasons that sexuality often goes unaddressed in disability services. Sexual expression has no practical applications and contributes nothing to a disabled person's independence. It furthers no career or educational goals. In the view of independence-minded clinicians, it is useless. The pursuit of the "highest level" of independence may thus have no room for sexuality, or may see it as a goal to be pursued after a client is considered fully independent by the relevant decision-makers—which may be never. In practice, this means that goals unrelated to self-sufficiency, including such not-readily-quantifiable goals as happiness and enjoyment, are often sacrificed. Think of this the next time you hear the word "independence" in your practice setting. Who chose that goal in the first place? Who will decide whether that goal is accomplished? Does your client have other self-defined goals and wishes that are being ignored in favor of a push for independence? None of this should be taken to mean that the concept of independence has no value in clinical practice—for many reasons, your clients might themselves choose to pursue goals that lead to greater self-sufficiency—but this drive toward independence should be based on what the client values, not on an arbitrary measuring stick that devalues those who depend on others. Furthermore, there are often better and more precise words to describe concepts related to independence. If you simply want to express your client's wish to make their own decisions and take control of their own lives, "autonomy" or "self-determination" are better word choices.

In that vein, pay additional attention to the way you talk about dependence, especially concerning the transfer of resources. Not only do we devalue people who are dependent on others, we also often assign the care efforts of disabled people a lower value than that of non-disabled people. In your practice, are you paying more attention to the flow of resources from able to disabled people than that from disabled people to able people, or between disabled people? Do you highly value the labor of able people who provide services and care to disabled people, but dismiss the (often unpaid and undervalued) contributions of disabled people? Leah Lakshmi Piepzna-Samarasinha, writing in *Bitch Media*, describes the ad-hoc, unofficial support networks of disabled people:

> [Y]our life as a working class or poor and/or sex working and/or disabled and/or Black or brown femme person has taught you that the only damn way you or anybody survives is by helping each other. No institutions exist to help us survive—we survive because of each other. Your life is maintained by a complex, non-monetary economy of shared, reciprocal care. You drop off some extra food; I listen to you when you're freaking out. You share your car with me; I pick you up from the airport. We pass the same twenty dollars back and forth between each

other, building movements and communities as we go. It's maybe what hippies mean when they talk about the gift economy, it's just a million times more working class, femme, Black and brown, and sick in bed.

(Piepzna-Samarasinha, 2017)

Peer support networks have the added benefit of being self-directed and administered by no particular authority. Peers are often able to offer kinds of help that are inaccessible from "official" sources, obtainable without the need to cut through layers of bureaucracy. This can be crucial when clients need services related to sexuality that are not easily justified to "official" sources of help. If one of your clients wants a ride to a sex toy shop or advice on kink relationships, they will be much more likely to ask a friend than a professional. Think about this the next time you hear someone praising the work of nonprofits and government agencies while ignoring the unglamorous work of peers. Think also about the value of peer relationships when you set out to help your clients build support networks.

The Language of Risk

Independence and autonomy closely relate to the concept of risk. If a person is considered autonomous and independent, we instinctively categorize them as bearing the risk burden of their decisions. If your able neighbor is determined to set off fireworks indoors, you may feel that you have little legal or ethical responsibility to prevent him from burning his house down. However, intellectually disabled people are often prevented from making decisions that could carry risk, typically by overzealous policies or simply the whims of a particular professional. The risk burden of their decisions is taken out of their hands and assigned to a clinician or caregiver, who may feel that the client is unable to appreciate the potential consequences of their actions. This may lead to others being inappropriately involved in decisions that are normally considered personal, or unilaterally vetoing decisions that carry even a small amount of risk. Engaging in sex or embarking on a gender transition always carries some amount of risk—condoms break, contraception fails, medical procedures have complications—but we somehow fail as professionals to realize that intellectually disabled people have the right to assume that risk.

Your practice setting may use the language of risk management around sexuality issues, suggesting subtly or overtly that your organization is responsible for any negative outcome of your clients' sexual decisions, perhaps with the additional fear of legal risk (though as you may recall from Chapter 3, there are also legal risks to ignoring clients' wishes). Risk management language sometimes has the effect both of making any potentially risky decision into a group decision, thus undermining a client's autonomy, and of making the organization unnecessarily risk-averse, attempting to dissuade the client from making decisions that most people consider ordinary. If sexuality- and gender identity-related decisions are considered "threats" to the client's well-being from a risk management perspective, it is inevitable that providers are going to view such decisions—and perhaps their clients' sexuality and gender identity in general—negatively. Richards and Fedoroff (2016) describe a case study in which an intellectually disabled person is rejected for gender-confirmation surgery solely due to their intellectual disability without even a cursory examination of the client's ability to understand their decision. This is strikingly common (though less so now than in the past), as providing intellectually disabled people with medical services related to gender transition is seen as a disproportionately great risk—both to the patient, who is presumed not to be able to understand the risk, and to the provider, who is seen as shouldering the entire responsibility of any negative consequences that result. Recall Cerridwyn in Chapter 5, whose conservatorship meant that her parents were involved in her gender-related medical decisions to an intrusive degree. At this point, Cerridwyn had more than demonstrated the ability to make responsible decisions autonomously, but her healthcare providers still insisted on speaking to her parents, sometimes without her. Though Cerridwyn protested this, these providers saw fit to take her decisions out of her hands in the name of caution.

Clearly, our thinking around risk management has to change to accommodate clients' sexual and gender autonomy. A helpful thought exercise is to force yourself to think of the risks of the client *not* being allowed to make their own decisions about sexuality and gender. This includes not only immediate risks, but chronic ones. A client whose caregivers prevent him from engaging in romantic relationships may be protected from sexually transmitted diseases and unwanted parenthood, but he may also come to feel that his life is incomplete without the chance to experience sex, physical affection, and the joys of coupledom. A trans client who is denied the opportunity to medically transition may be shielded from the possibility of regret or physical complications, but will likely be at increased risk of depression and suicide. Viewed in this way, the benefits of respecting these clients' decisions far outweigh the benefits of "protecting" them. Moreover, even if we do *not* feel that the benefits of their decisions outweigh the risks, we are not the ones who must bear their consequences.

Student vs. Teacher: the Role of Expertise

Many intellectually disabled people who receive disability-related services will receive such services to some degree throughout their lives. Unfortunately, this often places intellectually disabled people in the role of permanent student, with professionals in the role of "expert" or "teacher." Their "studenthood" can have the effect not only of preventing them from being trusted as the experts on their own lives, but of denying that their expertise could be of value to others. This is regrettable, as intellectually disabled people who have successfully dealt with sexuality and gender identity issues have a wealth of experience to share with peers and professionals. There is no better teacher than one who has struggled with and triumphed over the subject to be taught.

Fortunately, there are ways to channel the expertise of intellectually disabled people using your own professional resources. Frawley and Bigby (2014) describe a sexuality and relationship education program that was originally designed as a professionally led program, but was redesigned to include peer education. This proved to be an excellent addition, as the new peer educators proved more than up to the task of providing other intellectually disabled people with relationship education. Peer educators reported in their own words how important it was to them to have support from someone in similar circumstances:

> They can relate. . . . Like, I go to [other peer educator], um, as a person with a disability to a person with a disability . . . for help. . . . I have trouble dealing with [support worker] because she doesn't have a disability and I feel uncomfortable. I'd prefer to talk to [peer educator] because I know she's got a disability and I know she knows where I'm coming from. . . . [Y]ou get so much out of [peer education]. It's so worth it. Especially people with disabilities. There's no better way to get a message across from someone that you can relate to. . . . If you can relate to someone, you're going to listen to them.
>
> (Frawley & Bigby, 2014)

Unsurprisingly, some peer educators were apparently better able to understand and empathize with their peers' struggles than professionals were. Many peer educators reported hearing experiences from participants that resonated with their own. Distinct from the professional facilitators in the program, the peer educators were far better able to understand—viscerally and emotionally—what the participants had gone through. Speaking about an adult couple whose privacy was repeatedly violated by staff, one peer educator angrily stated:

> They ripped it [private sign] down on them. Like these [people with an intellectual disability] are grown adults, consenting adults. They don't need to be treated like they're children. And yeah, that really got on my nerves. I had to go home and cool down after hearing that. Yeah, I was quite grrr.
>
> (Frawley & Bigby, 2014)

Not only did the participants in the program learn from the experiences of their peer educators, the educators themselves reported that they had learned new skills and felt empowered by the experience (Frawley & Bigby, 2014). In addition, they helped the professionals around them understand the importance of peer education, imparting their expertise on those traditionally considered the "experts":

Well, I'll tell you what. When [the program manager] came with a [a peer educator] . . . just hearing [the peer educator] talk about her work, was sufficient for me to say what a benefit it would have been for [her] . . . . She spoke about her work and how important her work is for other people . . . to get other women empowered to stand up for themselves and [this is] what is achieved, not all the time, but most of the time. But her relaying of that . . . was so good for her was what shone for me.

Far from being "lesser" or auxiliary instructors, peer educators were vital to this program, turning an ordinary sex education program into a way for participants to get sexuality information and resources that they felt they could not normally ask of professionals. They "professionalized" themselves by using the resources and training of the organization administering the program, but remained accessible and approachable to their peers.

Peer education is just one way that authority and expertise can be democratized in matters of sexuality. However, it represents one of the more important ones, as intellectually disabled educators are the only people who can provide a direct, unfiltered view into their own lives. Peer education and support can be delivered in many formats, including over the internet. Appendix B lists blogs by peer advocates and educators.

The Issue With "Issues" and the Problem With "Problems"

In the introduction, we touched on the subject of "problems" and "issues": matters of sexuality and gender in clients that other professionals identify as "of concern." If you are the only person in your practice setting who regularly talks about sex and gender topics, you may be called upon to "solve" or "deal with" a wide range of concerns around client sexuality and gender. These might take the form of a client displaying sexual behaviors or dressing in gender-atypical clothing, identifying themselves using LGBTQ terms, or simply asking questions about sex. The problem comes when these behaviors are labeled as "problems"—or the less ominous but just as stigmatizing "issues." In my own practice, I regularly hear the term "gender identity issues," as if a trans person's gender identity is another item to tick off on a list of physical and mental health complaints. "Confusion" is another word that I hear often. This term stigmatizes clients who have a healthy amount of curiosity about their own and others' sexuality, and has the added effect of implying that LGBTQ identities are illegitimate: the products of ignorance or mistake rather than the client's true feelings. The unifying factor in all of these terms is the idea that sexuality and gender identity are clinical concerns no different than heart disease or diabetes. This places the clinician in the role of "resolving" the issue or performing an "intervention." Such an intervention may be unwelcome to the client, who may not conceive of their questions, identity, or behavior as problematic, or may merely hope for a friendly, open-ended discussion without the pressure to "resolve" anything in particular.

Alternatives to stigmatizing problem-based vocabulary are easy to come by. If a client asks questions that are complex and difficult to answer, simply say that the client has questions, not "issues" or "problems." The word "explore" is also a good way to talk about clients who have not settled on a fixed identity, as in "Bella is exploring the use of gender-neutral pronouns," which is much more accurate than using words related to confusion. Use words related to identity to talk about a client's feelings about their own sexuality and gender—as in, "Mark feels that he may identify as gay" versus "Mark is having sexuality issues"—and avoid using the type of terminology normally used to talk about disease and affliction. Unless a client's sexual behavior is dangerous or violates the rights of others, try not to imply that it is something that needs to be "solved" or "fixed" by a professional. If the client is in distress, it is fine to note this, but do not assume that a particular concern *must* cause the client distress without confirming this.

Apply Your Skills With Case Study #7: Carl

You are a social worker at a Q-Space, a small organization that provides free counseling and support groups to LGBTQ youth. You learn of a potential resource for staff education in your area: Carl, an autistic man who is involved in disability activism and conducts workshops designed to help nonprofits better serve clients on the autism spectrum. You bring this information to your manager, hoping to bring Carl in to lead a workshop with Q-Space's staff, who largely have no training in working with autistic clients, though your organization does serve a significant number of youth clients on the autism spectrum. Your manager sends an email to Carl, who does not respond for several days. You later learn that your manager asked Carl to conduct the workshop for free, though he lists his fee schedule on his web site and is quite clear that he charges for his services. You convince your manager to reach out again and offer Carl his typical fee, which your organization's budget can support. Carl agrees to hold a workshop next week for your staff. You and your manager speak with Carl on the morning of his workshop as he is setting up his presentation materials. During this brief conversation, your manager asks several intrusive questions about Carl's sexuality. Carl, who is openly gay, is visibly startled by her questions. Your manager also implies that Carl should have led the workshop for free and points out rather rudely that the organization helps many youth clients on the autism spectrum. The workshop turns out to be a success and your staff feels better equipped to serve autistic LGBTQ clients. However, you are embarrassed at your manager's behavior and don't want to repeat this experience with other outside training providers—or with your clients.

1. On whom does your manager place the burden of help- ing? Why does she feel Carl should have helped? Whom

does your manager feel should get *credit* for acts of helping? Why?

2. Why might your manager have felt permitted to ask Carl questions about his sexuality unprompted? Think about what your manager might believe about being a clinician or "expert."

3. What examples do you see in your own practice, or your own community, of unpaid labor by disabled people? What seems to be the deciding factor in whether someone is paid for their services?

4. Why is it important to solicit expertise from a disabled person like Carl rather than from an activist who is not disabled? What can he offer that non-disabled people can't?

Conclusion

The interventions described in this book represent only a fraction of the ways in which you can help your clients embrace the joyful variety of their sexuality and gender identity. You will find many opportunities to put this book's principles into practice, and plenty of other opportunities where your training fails you and you must seek out more resources. There is no substitute for experiencing these moments for yourself. This book is intended not just as an informational resource, but a call to action for you to stand up for your clients', students', and patients' sexual rights in your workplace. With luck, your clients will begin to seek you out for sexuality information, and you will find yourself paging through the book's resources and lending it to your coworkers.

It is my hope, moreover, that you will adopt the spirit in which the information is offered. Perhaps you may begin to look more critically at the ways in which our social and sexual worlds are built around the needs of people labeled "able" and whose differences from others are normalized and accommodated. If you identify yourself as able, you may also begin to look critically at the privilege your own identity affords you in navigating these social spaces. The effect that your actions as an able person have on others—not just clients, but your wider social sphere—may become more apparent through this lens. You will soon be spotting areas for improvement in your organization's practices that were never visible to you before.

The appendices that follow are essential reading for your professional education. They will allow you to learn more about sexuality topics for which your professional education may not have prepared you, and to access resources for your organization and clients around sexuality topics. Whatever your role or level of practice, you will be sure to find new information and expand your competence. In the spirit of the radical approach to disability, these resources have been selected with a focus on justice and inclusion, and represent the most up-to-date information available on their respective topics.

References

Advocates for Youth (2011). *National sexuality education standards: Core content and skills*. Retrieved September 28, 2017, from www.advocatesforyouth.org/publications/publications-a-z/1947-future-of-sex-education-national-sexuality-education-standards

Allen, J. D. (2003). *Gay, lesbian, bisexual, and transgender people with developmental disabilities and mental retardation: Stories of the Rainbow Support Group*. New York, NY: Routledge.

Azar, S. T., Stevenson, M. T., & Johnson, D. R. (2012). Intellectual disabilities and neglectful parenting: Preliminary findings on the role of cognition in parenting risk. *Journal of Mental Health Research in Intellectual Disabilities, 5*(2), 94–129. doi:10.1080/19315864.2011.615460

Balogh, R., Bretherton, K., Whibley, S., Berney, T., Graham, S., Richold, P., Worsley, C. & Firth, H. (2001). Sexual abuse in children and adolescents with intellectual disability. *Journal of Intellectual Disability Research, 45*(3), 194–201. doi:10.1046/j.1365-2788.2001.00293.x

Bennett, C., & Coyle, A. (2007). A minority within a minority: Experiences of gay men with intellectual disabilities. In *Out in Psychology: Lesbian, Gay, Bisexual, Trans and Queer Perspectives* (pp. 125–145). Hoboken, NJ: Wiley.

Bernert, D. J., & Ogletree, R. J. (2012, March 12). Women with intellectual disabilities talk about their perceptions of sex. *Journal of Intellectual Disability Research, 57*(3), 240–249. doi:10.1111/j.1365-2788.2011.01529.x

Booth, T., & Booth, W. (1997). *Growing up with parents who have learning difficulties*. New York, NY: Routledge.

Bowman, R. A., Scotti, J. R., & Morris, T. L. (2010). Sexual abuse prevention: A training program for developmental disabilities service providers. *Journal of Child Sexual Abuse, 19*(2), 119–127. doi:10.1080/10538711003614718

Brown, L. (n.d.). *Identity-first language*. Retrieved November 5, 2017, from http://autisticadvocacy.org/about-asan/identity-first-language/

Caldas, S. J., & Bensy, M. L. (2014). The sexual maltreatment of students with disabilities in American school settings. *Journal of Child Sexual Abuse, 23*(4), 345–366. doi:10.1080/10538712.2014.906530

California Evidence-Based Clearinghouse. (2015). *Healthy & safe*. Retrieved October 1, 2017, from www.cebc4cw.org/program/healthy-safe/

California Evidence-Based Clearinghouse. (2016). *Step-by-step parenting program©*. Retrieved October 1, 2017, from www.cebc4cw.org/program/step-by-step-parenting-program/

California Penal Code § 261 (1872).

Cambridge, P. (2012). A rights approach to supporting the sexual fetish of a man with learning disability: Method, process and applied learning. *British Journal of Learning Disabilities, 41*(4), 259–265. doi:10.1111/j.1468-3156.2012.00750.x

Chou, Y., Lu, Z. J., & Lin, C. (2016). Comparison of attitudes to the sexual health of men and women with intellectual disability among parents, professionals, and university students. *Journal of Intellectual & Developmental Disability*, 1–10. doi:10.3109/13668250.2016.1259465

Collings, S., & Llewellyn, G. (2012). Children of parents with intellectual disability: Facing poor outcomes or faring okay? *Journal of Intellectual and Developmental Disability, 37*(1), 65–82. doi:10.3109/13668250.2011.648610

Craig, L. A., & Hutchinson, R. B. (2005). Sexual offenders with learning disabilities: Risk, recidivism and treatment. *Journal of Sexual Aggression, 11*(3), 289–304. doi:10.1080/13552600500273919

Cruz, V. K., Price-Williams, D. R., & Andron, L. (1988). Developmentally disabled women who were molested as children. *Social Casework, 69*(7), 411-419.

Cuskelly, M., & Bryde, R. (2004). Attitudes towards the sexuality of adults with an intellectual disability: Parents, support staff, and a community sample. *Journal of Intellectual and Developmental Disability, 29*(3), 255–264. doi:10.1080/13668250412331285136

DeBellis, M. (2012). A group home exclusively for married couples with developmental disabilities: A natural next step. *Touro Law Review, 28*(2).

Degue, S., Valle, L. A., Holt, M. K., Massetti, G. M., Matjasko, J. L., & Tharp, A. T. (2014). A systematic review of primary prevention strategies for sexual violence perpetration. *Aggression and Violent Behavior, 19*(4), 346-362. doi:10.1016/j.avb.2014.05.004

DeWeerdt, S. (2017, May 18). The joys and challenges of being a parent with autism. *The Atlantic*. Retrieved from www.theatlantic.com/health/archive/2017/05/autism-parenting/526989/

Diament, M. (2014, April 22). Group homes' decision to bar Newlyweds from cohabiting upheld. *Disability Scoop*. Retrieved October 1, 2017, from www.disabilityscoop.com/2014/04/22/group-homes-cohabiting-upheld/19297/

Engber, D. (2015, October 24). *The strange case of Anna Stubblefield*. Retrieved October 1, 2017, from www.nytimes.com/2015/10/25/magazine/the-strange-case-of-anna-stubblefield.html

Feldman, M. A., & Case, L. (1999). Teaching child-care and safety skills to parents with intellectual disabilities through self-learning. *Journal of Intellectual and Developmental Disability, 24*(1), 27–44. doi:10.1080/13668259900033861

Fitzgerald, C., & Withers, P. (2011, November 28). 'I don't know what a proper woman means': What women with intellectual disabilities think about sex, sexuality and themselves. *British Journal of Learning Disabilities, 41*(1), 5–12. doi:10.1111/j.1468-3156.2011.00715.x

Frawley, P., & Bigby, C. (2014). "I'm in their shoes": Experiences of peer educators in sexuality and relationship education. *Journal of Intellectual and Developmental Disability, 39*(2), 167–176. doi:10.3109/13668250.2014.890701

Furries with aspergers/autism. (n.d.). Retrieved October 1, 2017, from http://forums.furaffinity.net/threads/furries-with-aspergers-autism.1254186/

Galea, J., Butler, J., Iacono, T., & Leighton, D. (2004). The assessment of sexual knowledge in people with intellectual disability. *Journal of Intellectual and Developmental Disability, 29*(4), 350–365. doi:10.1080/13668250400014517

Gilmore, L., & Chambers, B. (2010). Intellectual disability and sexuality: Attitudes of disability support staff and leisure industry employees. *Journal of Intellectual and Developmental Disability, 35*(1), 22–28. doi:10.3109/13668250903496344

Griffiths, D., Hingsburger, D., Hoath, J., & Ioannou, S. (2013). 'Counterfeit Deviance' revisited. *Journal of Applied Research in Intellectual Disabilities, 26*(5), 471–480. doi:10.1111/jar.12034

Hames, A. (1996). The effects of experience and sexual abuse training on the attitudes of learning disability staff. *Journal of Intellectual Disability Research, 40*(6), 544–549. doi:10.1046/j.1365-2788.1996.01313.x

Hogg, J., Campbell, M., Cullen, C., & Hudson, W. (2001). Evaluation of the effect of an open learning course on staff knowledge and attitudes towards the sexual abuse of adults with learning disabilities. *Journal of Applied Research in Intellectual Disabilities, 14*(1), 12–29. doi:10.1046/j.1468-3148.2001.00049.x

International Commission of Jurists. (2007, March). *The Yogyakarta principles: Principles on the application of International Human Rights Law in relation to sexual orientation and gender identity* (Rep.). Retrieved from www.yogyakartaprinciples.org/wp/wp-content/uploads/2016/08/principles_en.pdf

International Women's Health Coalition. (n.d.). *Sexual rights are human rights—IWHC*. Retrieved October 1, 2017, from http://iwhc.org/articles/sexual-rights-human-rights/

Jones, L., Bellis, M. A., Wood, S., Hughes, K., McCoy, E., Eckley, L., . . . Officer, A. (2012). Prevalence and risk of violence against children with disabilities: A systematic review and meta-analysis of observational studies. *The Lancet, 380*(9845), 899–907. doi:10.1016/s0140-6736(12)60692-8

Kaldera, R., & Tashlin, D. (2014). *Broken toys: Submissives with mental illness and neurological dysfunction*. Morrisville, NC: Lulu Press, Inc.

Ledger, S., Chapman, R., & Townson, L. (2014). Stories from Around the Globe. In *Sexuality and relationships in the lives of people with intellectual disabilities: Standing in my shoes* (pp. 26–33). London: Jessica Kingsley.

Lee, Y. K., & Tang, C. S. (1998). Evaluation of a sexual abuse prevention program for female Chinese adolescents with mild mental retardation. *American Journal on Mental Retardation, 103*(2), 105. doi:10.1352/0895-8017(1998)103<0105:eoasap>2.0.co;2

Lindsay, W. R. (2002). Research and literature on sex offenders with intellectual and developmental disabilities. *Journal of*

Intellectual Disability Research, 46(S1), 74–85. doi:10.1046/j.1365-2788.2002.00006.x

Lockhart, K., Guerin, S., Shanahan, S., & Coyle, K. (2010). Expanding the test of counterfeit deviance: Are sexual knowledge, experience and needs a factor in the sexualised challenging behaviour of adults with intellectual disability? *Research in Developmental Disabilities, 31*(1), 117–130. doi:10.1016/j.ridd.2009.08.003

Mansell, S., Sobsey, D., & Calder, P. (1992). Sexual abuse treatment for persons with developmental disabilities. *Professional Psychology: Research and Practice, 23*(5), 404–409. doi:10.1037//0735-7028.23.5.404

Mary H. Kortner, Administratrix (Estate of Caroline Kendall Kortner) v. Craig L. Martise. (2014, June 10).

McBrien, J., Hodgetts, A., & Gregory, J. (2003). Offending and risky behaviour in community services for people with intellectual disabilities in one local authority. *Journal of Forensic Psychiatry & Psychology, 14*(2), 280–297. doi:10.1080/1478994031000084828

McCarthy, M., Hunt, S., & Milne-Skillman, K. (2016). 'I know it was every week, but I can't be sure if it was every day: Domestic violence and women with learning disabilities. *Journal of Applied Research in Intellectual Disabilities, 30*(2), 269–282. doi:10.1111/jar.12237

McCarthy, M., & Thompson, D. (1996). Sexual abuse by design: An examination of the issues in learning disability services. *Disability & Society, 11*(2), 205–218. doi:10.1080/09687599650023236

McClelland, A., Flicker, S., Nepveux, D., Nixon, S., Vo, T., Wilson, C., . . . Proudfoot, D. (2012). Seeking safer sexual spaces: Queer and trans young people labeled with intellectual disabilities and the paradoxical risks of restriction. *Journal of Homosexuality, 59*(6), 808–819. doi:10.1080/00918369.2012.694760

McCormack, B., Kavanagh, D., Caffrey, S., & Power, A. (2005). Investigating sexual abuse: Findings of a 15-year longitudinal study. *Journal of Applied Research in Intellectual Disabilities, 18*(3), 217–227. doi:10.1111/j.1468-3148.2005.00236.x

McEachern, A. G. (2012). Sexual abuse of individuals with disabilities: Prevention strategies for clinical practice. *Journal of Child Sexual Abuse, 21*(4), 386–398. doi:10.1080/10538712.2012.675425

McGrath, R. J., Livingston, J. A., & Falk, G. (2007). Community management of sex offenders with intellectual disabilities:

Characteristics, services, and outcome of a statewide program. *Intellectual and Developmental Disabilities, 45*(6), 391–398. doi:10.1352/1934-9556(2007)45[391:cmosow]2.0.co;2

McKelvey, R. S., Webb, J. A., Baldassar, L. V., Robinson, S. M., & Riley, G. (1999). Sex knowledge and sexual attitudes among medical and nursing students. *Australian & New Zealand Journal of Psychiatry, 33*(2), 260–266. doi:10.1046/j.1440-1614.1999.00549.x

McNeill Profound mental disabilities [Web post].

Meaney-Tavares, R., & Gavidia-Payne, S. (2012). Staff characteristics and attitudes towards the sexuality of people with intellectual disability. *Journal of Intellectual and Developmental Disability, 37*(3), 269–273. doi:10.3109/13668250.2012.701005

Michie, A. M., Lindsay, W. R., Martin, V., & Grieve, A. (2006). A test of counterfeit deviance: A comparison of sexual knowledge in groups of sex offenders with intellectual disability and controls. *Sexual Abuse: A Journal of Research and Treatment, 18*(3), 271–278. doi:10.1177/107906320601800305

Miller, D., & Brown, J. (2014, October). *'We have the right to be safe': Protecting disabled children from abuse* (Rep.). Retrieved www.nspcc.org.uk/globalassets/documents/research-reports/right-safe-disabled-children-abuse-report.pdf

Miller, L. (2016, January 24). Who knows best. *The Cut*. Retrieved October 1, 2017, from www.thecut.com/2016/01/how-intelligent-to-be-a-parent.html

Miller, W. R., & Rollnick, S. (1991). *Motivational interviewing: Preparing people to change addictive behavior*. New York, NY: Guilford Press.

Nabehet, R. (2014, July 9). 5 realities of being raised by an intellectually handicapped parent. *Thought Catalog*. Retrieved October 1, 2017, from http://thoughtcatalog.com/roseminda-nabehet/2014/07/5-realities-of-being-raised-by-an-intellectually-handicapped-parent/

Nagoski, E. (2014, July 11). *An awesome question: Is there a link between Autism spectrum and BDSM?* [Web log post]. Retrieved October 1, 2017, from www.thedirtynormal.com/blog/2014/07/11/an-awesome-question-aspergers-and-bdsm/

National Council on Disability. (2012, September 27). *Rocking the cradle: Ensuring the rights of parents with disabilities and their children*. Retrieved October 1, 2017, from http://ncd.gov/publications/2012/Sep272012

Piepzna-Samarasinha, L. L. (2017, July 13). A modest proposal for a fair trade emotional labor economy. *Bitch Media*. Retrieved from www.bitchmedia.org/article/modest-proposal-fair-trade-emotional-labor-economy/centered-disabled-femme-color-working

Pinciaro, J. (2013a, July 2). Married couple living together—finally. *Patch*. Retrieved October 1, 2017, from http://patch.com/new-york/riverhead/married-couple-living-together--finally

Pinciaro, J. (2013b, July 17). Disabled couple's lawsuit appears closer to trial. *Patch*. Retrieved October 1, 2017, from http://patch.com/new-york/portjefferson/disabled-couples-lawsuit-appears-closer-to-trial

Plante, C. N., Roberts, S. E., Reysen, S., & Gerbasi, K. C. (2013). *International anthropomorphic research project: Anthrocon 2013 summary*. Retrieved October 1, 2017, from International Anthropomorphic Research Project: Anthrocon 2013 Summary.

Pohl, A., Crockford, S., Blakemore, M., Allison, C., & Baron-Cohen, S. (2016, May 14). *Positive & negative experiences of 325 autistic mothers vs 91 typical mothers, online survey 'autism and motherhood'*. Retrieved October 30, 2017, from www.autismwomenmatter.org.uk/research/positive-negative-experiences-of-325-autistic-mothers-vs-91-typical-mothers-online-survey-autism-and-motherhood/

Profound mental disabilities [Web post]. (2011, September 15). Retrieved October 1, 2017, from http://maggiemcneill.wordpress.com/2011/09/15/profound-mental-disabilities/

/r/AskReddit. (n.d.). *Doctors of reddit, what's something you've had to tell a patient that you thought for sure was common knowledge?* Retrieved October 1, 2017, from www.reddit.com/r/AskReddit/comments/27p6z3/doctors_of_reddit_whats_something_youve_had_to/

Richards, D. A., & Fedoroff, J. P. (2016). Helping those with intellectual disabilities. In *Handbook of clinical sexuality for mental health professionals* (pp. 250–262). New York, NY: Routledge.

Rose, J., Jenkins, R., O'Connor, C., Jones, C., & Felce, D. (2002). A group treatment for men with intellectual disabilities who sexually offend or abuse. *Journal of Applied Research in Intellectual Disabilities, 15*(2), 138–150. doi:10.1046/j.1468-3148.2002.00110.x

Rose, N., Rose, J., & Kent, S. (2012). Staff training in intellectual disability services: A review of the literature and implications for mental health services provided to individuals with intellectual disability. *International Journal of Developmental Disabilities, 58*(1), 24–39. doi :10.1179/2047387711y.0000000005

Salazar, L. F., Vivolo-Kantor, A., Hardin, J., & Berkowitz, A. (2014). A web-based sexual violence bystander intervention for male college students: Randomized controlled trial. *Journal of Medical Internet Research, 16*(9). doi:10.2196/jmir.3426

Schaafsma, D., Kok, G., Stoffelen, J. M., & Curfs, L. M. (2014). Identifying effective methods for teaching sex education to individuals with intellectual disabilities: A systematic review. *The Journal of Sex Research, 52*(4), 412–432. doi:10.1080/00224499.2014.919373

Schaafsma, D., Kok, G., Stoffelen, J. M., Doorn, P. V., & Curfs, L. M. (2014). Identifying the important factors associated with teaching sex education to people with intellectual disability: A cross-sectional survey among paid care staff. *Journal of Intellectual and Developmental Disability, 39*(2), 157–166. doi:10.3109/13668250.2 014.899566

Sex Offender Treatment Services Collaborative-Intellectual Disabilities (SOTSEC-ID). (2010). Effectiveness of group cognitive-behavioural treatment for men with intellectual disabilities at risk of sexual offending. *Journal of Applied Research in Intellectual Disabilities, 23*(6), 537–551. doi:10.1111/j.1468-3148.2010.00560.x

Sexual Rights Initiative. (n.d.). *Intro to sexual rights.* Retrieved October 1, 2017, from www.sexualrightsinitiative.com/sexual-rights/intro-to-sexual-rights/

Shahbaz, C., & Chirinos, P. (2017). *Becoming a kink aware therapist.* New York, NY: Routledge.

Smith, S. E. (n.d.). Apparently, if you're disabled, the state can decide whether you're allowed to live with your spouse.

Snow, K. (2016). Interdependence. *Disability is Natural,* Disability is Natural Books and Media. Retrieved from www.disabilityisnatural. com/interdependence.html

Stalker, K., & McArthur, K. (2010). Child abuse, child protection and disabled children: A review of recent research. *Child Abuse Review, 21*(1), 24–40. doi:10.1002/car.1154

Thompson, V. R., Stancliffe, R. J., Broom, A., & Wilson, N. J. (2014). Barriers to sexual health provision for people with intellectual disability:

A disability service provider and clinician perspective. *Journal of Intellectual and Developmental Disability*, *39*(2), 137–146. doi:10.31 09/13668250.2014.898742

Thompson, V. R., Stancliffe, R. J., Broom, A., & Wilson, N. J. (2016). Clinicians' use of sexual knowledge assessment tools for people with intellectual disability. *Journal of Intellectual & Developmental Disability*, *41*(3), 243–254. doi:10.3109/13668250.2016.1164303

Tregaskis, C. (2004). *Constructions of disability: Researching the interface between disabled and non-disabled people.* London: Routledge.

United States, U.S. Department of Health and Human Services, Centers for Disease Control and Prevention. (2007). *Preventing Child Sexual Abuse Within Youth-serving Organizations: Getting Started on Policies and Procedures.*

Ward, K. M., Atkinson, J. P., Smith, C. A., & Windsor, R. (2013). A friendships and dating program for adults with intellectual and developmental disabilities: A formative evaluation. *Intellectual and Developmental Disabilities*, *51*(1), 22–32. doi:10.1352/1934-9556-51.01.022

Wells, S. (Director/Producer). (2008). *Sex and relationship education: Pioneering work on SRE at Shepherd School in Nottingham* [Video file]. United Kingdom: Teachers TV. Retrieved October 1, 2017, from www.creativeeducation.co.uk/video/1735

Wilson, N. J., & Frawley, P. (2016). Transition staff discuss sex education and support for young men and women with intellectual and developmental disability. *Journal of Intellectual & Developmental Disability*, *41*(3), 209–221. doi:10.3109/13668250.2016.1162771

Withers, A. (2014). *Radical model.* Retrieved September 28, 2017, from http://stillmyrevolution.org/2012/01/01/radical-model/

Wurtele, S. K. (1990). Teaching personal safety skills to four-year-old children: A behavioral approach. *Behavior Therapy*, *21*(1), 25–32. doi:10.1016/s0005-7894(05)80186-8

Wurtele, S. K., & Miller-Perrin, C. L. (1987). An evaluation of side effects associated with participation in a child sexual abuse prevention program. *Journal of School Health*, *57*(6), 228–231. doi:10.1111/j.1746-1561.1987.tb07838.x

Wurtele, S. K., & Owens, J. S. (1997). Teaching personal safety skills to young children: An investigation of age and gender across five studies. *Child Abuse & Neglect*, *21*(8), 805–814. doi:10.1016/s0145-2134(97)00040-9

Appendix A

Staff and Student Training and Information Resources

Web sites that offer **sexuality information and training resources** for professionals and students in healthcare, social services, and education include the following:

- The Institute for Sexual Health's web site provides information about physical and mental health issues relating to sex: www.sexualmed.org/
- The Society for the Scientific Study of Sexuality provides events and resources on sexuality topics for professionals: www.sexscience.org/
- The American Association of Sexuality Educators, Counselors, and Therapists holds an annual conference and provides accreditation for institutions that educate sex educators/therapists. Information on the organization's approved educational providers can be found at www.aasect.org/certification
- The World Health Organization (WHO) publishes a variety of guides on reproductive and sexual health topics from a global perspective: www.who.int/reproductivehealth/publications/en/
- UCSF's Center of Excellence for Transgender Health provides information about transgender health for healthcare providers and the general public: www.transhealth.ucsf.edu/
- The National LGBT Health Education Center has articles, courses, webinars, and online learning modules for healthcare and health education professionals on LGBTQ

topics, including a wealth of information on trans and non-binary identities: www.lgbthealtheducation.org/lgbt-education/

◆ The World Professional Association for Transgender Health (WPATH) provides training resources and certification for transgender healthcare providers, and includes a function to search for providers, which may be useful to trans clients: www.wpath.org/

Those wishing to learn more about **BDSM and kink** can visit the following sites:

◆ BDSM 101, a guide for BDSM novices, can be found at www.bdsm-101.com/
◆ The Pervocracy is a fun and informational blog on kink topics that can be read at www.pervocracy.blogspot.com/
◆ A Submissive's Journey offers a directory of information about a wide variety of BDSM/kink topics at www.asubmissivesjourney.com/page2.html
◆ WikiFur provides an extensive collection of encyclopedia articles about the furry fandom: www.en.wikifur.com/wiki/WikiFur_Furry_Central
◆ The Body Modification Ezine provides a wealth of information about body modification, including photographs. While not everyone who engages in body modification identifies it as a kink or sexual interest, many do, and others use body modification as a way of confirming or exploring their gender identity. Some physically disabled people report that using body modification to take control of their bodies and/or improve their body image. Warning: the images on the web site can be quite graphic. www.bme.com/

Information about **making HIV education accessible** for intellectually disabled people can be found in *Guidelines for Inclusion of Individuals with Disability in HIV/AIDS Outreach Efforts*, published by the World Bank: www.ucl.ac.uk/lc-ccr/

downloads/hivguidelines/HIV_Guidelines_on_Disability_-_World_Bank_-_ENGLIS.pdf

The **video about sex education** at the Shepherd School referenced in Chapter 1 can be found at www.creativeeducation.co.uk/video/1735. This web site also features several potentially useful informational videos on sex education topics.

A **documentary about intellectually disabled mothers** called *Different Moms* can be accessed by contacting Moxie Firecracker Films, whose contact information can be found at www.moxiefirecracker.com/

The National Sexual Violence Resource Center maintains a list of **educational resources** for staff of agencies that serve intellectually disabled people: www.nsvrc.org/projects/child-sexual-assault-prevention/preventing-child-sexual-abuse-resources

The CDC **guidelines on sexual abuse training** for staff can be found at www.cdc.gov/violenceprevention/pdf/preventing-childsexualabuse-a.pdf. This guide also lists resources on where to find **sample abuse prevention policies**.

Another **sample policy** for abuse prevention can be found via the New York State Justice Center for the Protection of People with Special Needs: www.justicecenter.ny.gov/node/1786.

Appendix B

Educational Materials for Intellectually Disabled Clients

The **sex education teaching materials** mentioned in Chapter 1 can be found at the following online locations:

- ◆ The Circles Curriculum can be purchased for $499 and up at www.stanfield.com/product/circles-curriculum-bundle-w1037-3/
- ◆ BodySense anatomically correct dolls may be purchased at www.bodysense.org.uk/
- ◆ The *Ellie* and *Tom* series of books can be found by visiting the Jessica Kingsley Publishers web site and searching their respective titles: www.jkp.com/index.php?uk
- ◆ CHANGE's sexuality and gender booklets can be purchased at www.changepeople.org/shop/products

Web sites for **general sex education** for clients (which may also be of use to staff who are looking for basic sexuality information for themselves) include the following, which generally require some degree of literacy to access, though the accessibility and complexity of the language used varies greatly:

- ◆ AMAZE, a web site operated by Advocates for Youth, provides animated videos about sexuality and gender topics, including many about LGBTQ identities. Since the medium is mostly audiovisual and the site has little text, it may be useful for clients with a lower degree of literacy. The site is available in English, Spanish, and French. www.amaze.org/

- Scarleteen is an excellent, accessible site for teens and young adults about sexuality, gender identity, and health: www.scarleteen.com/
- iwannaknow is the American Sexual Health Association's web site for teens and young adults, and features a wealth of sexual health information, including resources on LGBTQ identities: www.iwannaknow.org/
- Go Ask Alice! is a web site run by the Alice! Health Promotion Program at Columbia University, which provides thousands of answers to common (and uncommon) questions about sexual health: www.goaskalice.columbia.edu/
- Planned Parenthood's web site for teens provides basic information about sexuality with a focus on reproductive health, and includes quizzes and games: www.plannedparenthood.org/learn/teens
- Sex, Etc. provides fun, interesting articles about sex topics of interest to teenagers and young adults: www.sexetc.org/
- Quierosaber provides articles about sexuality for adults and adolescents in Spanish: www.quierosaber.org/
- On Safersex.Education (itself an excellent resource), Katie McCombs showcases five humorous and educational sex ed videos from YouTube, primarily intended for adults: www.safersex.education/kate-mccombs-6-sex-ed-videos-i-love/

Copies of two of the **Step-by-Step Parenting Program** manuals mentioned in Chapter 4 can be found by writing to Maurice Feldman at Brock University whose contact information can be found at www.brocku.ca/social-sciences/departments-and-centres/centre-for-applied-disability/faculty/maurice-feldman. The third can be obtained from NADD Press at www.thenadd.org/

Information about accessing the **Healthy & Safe** parenting program curriculum can be found on the web site of Healthy Start, an organization devoted to the needs of intellectually disabled parents: www.healthystart.net.au/index.php/for-professionals/programs-support. Note that, as it is an Australian program, some of the consultation resources found on Healthy Start's web site may not be available in the U.S. or other countries.

The Center for Parent Information and Resources provides a list of **sexuality education resources** for disabled children, adolescents, and adults and their families: www.parentcenterhub.org/sexed/

A list of **blogs by autistic people,** many of whom blog about sexuality and LGBTQ issues, can be found at www.anautismob server.wordpress.com/. The list is maintained by an autistic woman named Judy, who writes under the name An Autism Observer.

Kirsten Lindsmith, an author and autism advocate, writes thoughtfully about **autism, gender, sexuality,** and other topics at her blog, The Artism Spectrum: www.kirstenlindsmith.wordpress.com

Gillan Drew **blogs about parenting with Asperger Syndrome** at his web site Aspie Daddy: www.asdaddy.com/. Drew is also the author of the book *An Adult with an Autism Diagnosis: A Guide for the Newly Diagnosed.*

Casey Morton, a father with Mosaic Down Syndrome, **talks about parenting and relationships** in an interview with Psychology Today: www.psychologytoday.com/blog/imperfect-offerings/201002/the-inclusive-love-casey-and-shana

Appendix C
National Resources for Sexuality and Gender Identity Needs

Faculty at the University of British Columbia have published *PleasureAble*, a guide to **assistive devices** for physically disabled people. It can be found at www.dhrn.ca/files/sexualhealth manual_lowres_2010_0208.pdf

IntimateRider is a for-profit company that designs and manufactures **sexual assistive furniture and other devices** for physically disabled people, including the IntimateRider assistive chair pictured in Chapter 1. Their products can be purchased online at www.intimaterider.com/product/

Liberator is another company that makes **assistive furniture and pillows**, among other sexual wellness aids. Though these are not primarily designed for disabled people, they can be used to make sexual positioning easier. Their products can be found at www.liberator.com/

A video by sex educator Erika Lynae gives details on the use of **sex toys for physically disabled people**: www.erikalynae. com/2016/10/21/sex-toys-disability/

The American Bar Association's Commission on Disability Rights can be a good source of **legal information and resources** for disabled people: www.americanbar.org/groups/ disabilityrights.html

The Arc, an organization dedicated to serving intellectually disabled people, can be a source of **information and referrals on legal and other topics**. Find your local chapter at www.thearc. org/find-a-chapter

PFLAG provides **support and resources for families of LGBTQ people**. Find a local chapter and locate resources for families and individuals at www.pflag.org/needsupport

The Trevor Project provides **crisis counseling and hotline support for LGBTQ youth** across the United States. The organization also provides trainings for youth-serving professionals for a fee. Youth needing support can call their hotline at 1-866-488-7386, and the organization's web site can be found at www.thetrevorproject.org/

The Gay, Lesbian, Bisexual, and Transgender National Hotline provides **crisis support for LGBTQ people** of all ages. Visit them online at www.glbthotline.org/hotline.html. Those needing support can call 1-888-843-4564. Their number for youth up to age 25 is 1-800-246-7743.

Planned Parenthood provides a wide variety of **sexual health and wellness services** to people of all ages and abilities, including LGBTQ resources and support groups: www.plannedparenthood.org/get-care/our-services

The National Center for Transgender Equality provides **information on legal name changes** for transgender people at www.transequality.org/id-documents-center. The organization also maintains the Trans Legal Services Network, an extensive network of legal assistance providers that provide various **free and low-cost legal services** to trans people: www.transequality.org/issues/resources/trans-legal-services-network-directory

Dress For Success is an organization that provides free **interview clothing and workwear** to low-income and homeless women, which may be of interest to transfeminine clients with limited clothing resources: www.dressforsuccess.org/

Though there is no national equivalent to Dress For Success for men, many cities have local organizations that fulfill this function. For example, New York has Career Gear, an organization that provides **interview clothing and workwear** to low-income men referred by community partners: www.careergear.org/

The web site Homeless Needs provides a directory of local **clothing resources** in many states that trans clients with limited resources may find useful: www.homelessneeds.org/clothing/

The Association for the Treatment of Sexual Abusers provides referrals to **sexual abuser treatment providers**. Their online referral request form provides specifiers for intellectually disabled people. www.atsa.com/referral

The Safer Society Foundation maintains an extensive list of **sexual abuser treatment providers** as well as clinicians who provide **treatment for victims of sexual abuse**. The society's online listings include specifiers for providers that work with intellectually disabled people. www.safersociety.org/press/treatment-referrals/

Index